Quick Steps to Financial Stability

Alan Lavine and
Gail Liberman

800 East 96th Street,
Indianapolis, Indiana 46290

Quick Steps to Financial Stability

Copyright © 2007 by Alan Lavine and Gail Liberman

All rights reserved. No part of this book shall be reproduced, stored in a retrieval system, or transmitted by any means, electronic, mechanical, photocopying, recording, or otherwise, without written permission from the publisher. No patent liability is assumed with respect to the use of the information contained herein. Although every precaution has been taken in the preparation of this book, the publisher and author assume no responsibility for errors or omissions. Nor is any liability assumed for damages resulting from the use of the information contained herein.

International Standard Book Number: 0-7897-3508-3

Printed in the United States of America

First Printing: November 2006

09 08 07 06   4 3 2 1

Trademarks

All terms mentioned in this book that are known to be trademarks or service marks have been appropriately capitalized. Que Publishing cannot attest to the accuracy of this information. Use of a term in this book should not be regarded as affecting the validity of any trademark or service mark.

Warning and Disclaimer

Every effort has been made to make this book as complete and as accurate as possible, but no warranty or fitness is implied. The information provided is on an "as is" basis. The authors and the publisher shall have neither liability nor responsibility to any person or entity with respect to any loss or damages arising from the information contained in this book.

Bulk Sales

Que Publishing offers excellent discounts on this book when ordered in quantity for bulk purchases or special sales. For more information, please contact

    U.S. Corporate and Government Sales
    1-800-382-3419
    corpsales@pearsontechgroup.com

For sales outside the United States, please contact

    International Sales
    international@pearsoned.com

        Library of Congress Cataloging-in-Publication Data

Lavine, Alan.
  Quick steps to financial stability / Alan Lavine and Gail Liberman.
    p. cm.
  Includes bibliographical references and index.
  ISBN 0-7897-3508-3 (pbk. : alk. paper)
1. Finance, Personal. I. Liberman, Gail, 1951- II. Title.
  HG179.L3376 2007
  332.024'01—dc22
                2006027769

Associate Publisher
Greg Wiegand

Acquisitions Editor
Loretta Yates

Development Editor
Lorna Gentry

Managing Editor
Patrick Kanouse

Project Editor
Tonya Simpson

Copy Editor
Bill McManus

Indexer
Ken Johnson

Proofreader
Jessica McCarty

Technical Editor
Joe Thoma

Publishing Coordinator
Cindy Teeters

Book Designer
Anne Jones

CONTENTS AT A GLANCE

Introduction 1

Part I Are You Ready?
1. Examining Your Financial Condition 7
2. Identifying Your Financial Goals 23
3. Zeroing In on Your Debt 33

Part II Creating a Simple Investment Plan
4. Weighing the Pros and Cons of Simple Investment Options 51
5. Creating a Plan that Works for You 61
6. Protecting the Downside: Insurance and Other Safeguards 77

Part III Supercharging Your Savings Plan
7. Saving for Retirement 95
8. How to Pay for Your Children's Education 109
9. Save by Choosing the Right Loans 121
10. Your Keys to the Good Life, Now and Later 137

Part IV Appendixes
A. References and Resources 147
B. Finding the Right Help 157
C. Mortgage Shopping Worksheet 163
Index 169

Table of Contents

Introduction 1

What *Quick Steps to Financial Stability* Can Do for You 2

How This Book Is Organized 2

Special Elements and Icons 3
    To Do Lists 3
    Special Icons 4

I Are You Ready?

1 Examining Your Financial Condition 7

Net Worth: Finding Your Bottom Line 8
    Step 1: Round Up Your Assets 9
    Step 2: List All Your Liabilities or Debts 10
    Step 3: Subtract Your Liabilities from Your Assets 11

Reviewing Income and Expenses 11
    Step 1: Calculate Your Monthly Income 12
    Step 2: Categorize Monthly Expenses 13
    Step 3: Determine Where You Stand 15

Setting Your Financial Goals 15

Freeing Up Quick Cash 16
    Controlling Your Debt 17
    Trimming Expenses 17
    Beefing Up Your Income 20

Summary 21

2 Identifying Your Financial Goals 23

Preparing for Life 23
    Identifying Your Insurance Needs 24
    Setting Financial Goals 25
    Considering Your Savings Plan 26

Planning for Big Goals 28
    Buying a Home 28
    Having a Baby 30
    Saving for Your Children's Education and Retirement 32

Summary 32

3 Zeroing In on Your Debt 33

    Over Your Head in Debt? Try These Fixes 34
        Controlling Debt Yourself 35
        Credit Counseling 36
        Consolidating Your Debts 37
        Bankruptcy 38

    Understanding Your Credit Score 39
        Getting Your Score 40
        Check Your Credit Report to Raise Your Credit Score 42
        Correcting Mistakes on Your Credit Report 44
        What If Your Bad Credit Score Is Accurate? 45

    Summary 46

II Creating a Simple Investment Plan

4 Weighing the Pros and Cons of Simple Investment Options 51

    Understanding Basic Investments 52
        Cash 52
        Bonds 53
        Stocks 54
        Basic Investment Rules 54

    What Kind of Investor Are You? 56

    Investing in Mutual Funds and Exchange-Traded Funds 59

    Summary 60

5 Creating a Plan That Works for You 61

    Choose Low-Risk Investments for Short-Term Goals 62
        Bank Deposits 62
        U.S. Treasury Securities 64
        Other Lower-risk Investments 65

    Stocks: More Risk for Better Long-Term Returns 67

    Choose Mutual Funds to Help You Diversify 68
        Analyzing the Risk of Mutual Funds 68
        Pinpoint Your Strategy with Life-Cycle and Target Funds 69
        Take a More Conservative Approach with Balanced Funds 70

    Boost Your Performance 70
        Stick with No-Load Funds 70
        Use Index Funds 72

        Opting for Actively Managed Funds 72
        Consider Dollar Cost Averaging 73
        Rebalance Your Investments 73

    Always Consider Taxes 74

    Summary 75

6 Protecting the Downside: Insurance and Other Safeguards 77

    Finding Financially Secure Companies. 78

    Health Insurance 79
        Policy Types 80
        What to Examine Before Buying a Policy 81
        Cut the Cost of Medical Insurance 81

    Disability Insurance 82

    Life Insurance 84
        Low-Load Companies 86
        Getting Professional Help 86

    Long-Term Care Insurance 87

    Property Insurance 88
        Automobile Insurance 88
        Homeowner's Insurance 89

    You Need a Will. 90

    Summary 91

III Supercharging Your Savings Plan

7 Saving for Retirement. 95

    Determine What to Expect from Your Retirement Income Sources 96

    Your Retirement Plan Options 97
        401(k) 98
        IRAs. 99
        Roth IRA. 100
        Annuities. 101

    Can You Retire? 103
        Need More?. 106
        Other Ways to Retire 106

    Summary 107

8 How to Pay for Your Children's Education **109**

Getting Your Hands Around the Cost of College 110

Step 1: Determine What You Can Save 111

Step 2: Examine Your Investment Options 111
    529 Plans 111
    Coverdell Educational Savings Accounts 113
    Uniform Transfers to Minors Act and Uniform Gifts to Minors Act 113
    Other Tax-Advantaged Options 114

Tax Breaks for College Savings 114
    The Hope Scholarship Credit 115
    The Lifetime Learning Credit 115
    Tax Deduction for Student Loan Interest 115

Rules for College Investing 115

Financial Aid 116

If You Must Borrow 118

Other Ways to Get Your Children to College 118

Summary 119

9 Save by Choosing the Right Loans **121**

Your Loan Objectives 121

The Scoop on Credit Cards 122

Understanding Car Loans and Leases 124

Picking a Mortgage 126
    Checking Out Loan Upfront Costs and Fees 126
    Choosing a Mortgage Type 127
    Finding Information on Special Mortgage Programs 130

Home Equity Loans and Lines 131

Other Low-Cost Ways to Borrow 131

Beware When You Borrow Money 132

Eliminating Debt from Your Financial Life 133
    Refinance Your Home 133
    Prepay Your Mortgage 134
    Consider a Biweekly Mortgage 135

Summary 135

10 Your Keys to the Good Life, Now and Later 137

    Evaluate Your Income and Spending 138

    Evaluate Your Insurance Coverage 139

    Review Your Investments 140

    Review Your Tax Situation 140

    Update Your Estate Plan 141

    Enjoy Your Great New Financial Life 143

    Summary 143

IV Appendixes

A References and Resources 147

    Online Calculators 147
        Net Worth Calculator 148
        Goal Calculator 148
        College Cost Calculators 148
        Retirement Savings Calculators 148
        Home Loan or Home Buying Calculators 148
        Disability Insurance 148

    Search Engines 149

    Low Down-Payment and Low-Cost Government Mortgage Programs 149

    Credit Card Best Deals 149

    Money Market Mutual Fund Yields 149

    Scholarships and Loan Sources 149
        529 College Savings Plans 150

    Reverse Mortgage Information 150

    Taxes 150

    New and Used Car Prices 150
        Consumer Reports 150

    Car Leasing 151

    Home Buying 151

Attorneys 151
   Elder Law 151
   Consumer Law 151
   Marital Law 151

Low-Load Life Insurance 151

COBRA Insurance Information 152

Insurance Safety Rating Agencies 152

No-Load Mutual Fund Families 152

Mutual Funds Information and Analysis 152

Purchase U.S. Treasury Securities 152

Check for Complaints Against a Person or Business 152

Credit Reports and Credit Scoring 153
   Consumer Credit Reporting Agencies 153
   Largest Credit Scoring Provider 153

Help with Debt 153

Bankruptcy Information 153

Fraud 154

Insurance Information 154

Social Security Administration 154

Unclaimed Property 154

Consumer Expenditures 154

Economic Statistics and Salary Data 154

Financial Regulators 154

B Finding the Right Help **157**

Getting Good Investment Help 158

Getting Credit Counseling 159

C Mortgage Shopping Worksheet **163**

Index **169**

About the Authors

Gail Liberman and Alan Lavine are husband-and-wife columnists and best-selling authors based in Palm Beach Gardens, Florida.

Their columns run on Dow Jones MarketWatch and in the *Boston Herald*, *Pittsburgh Post-Gazette*, several Scripps Howard newspapers, MyFinancialAdvisor.com, Fundsinteractive.com, Allaboutfunds.com, and Quicken.com.

Liberman and Lavine's book *Rags to Riches: Motivating Stories of How Ordinary People Achieved Extraordinary Wealth!* (Dearborn, 2000) was featured on *Oprah* and hit two best-seller lists.

You might have seen or heard the couple on television and radio. They have been guests on CBS's *The Early Show*, CNN, CNBC, *The 700 Club*, NBC, Fox, and PBS. They also have been quoted in *The Wall Street Journal, Money Magazine, USA Today*, the *New York Times, Business Week, Investor's Business Daily, The Washington Post, Redbook, First, Town and Country, Bride's,* and *Elle*.

Their other books are *The Complete Idiot's Guide to Making Money with Mutual Funds* (Alpha Books, 2000), *Rags to Retirement* (Alpha Books, 2003), *More Rags to Riches* (Dearborn, 2002), *Love, Marriage and Money* (Dearborn, 1998), *Improving Your Credit and Reducing Your Debt* (Wiley, 1994), *Short and Simple Guide to Life Insurance* (Authors Choice, 2000), and *Short and Simple Guide to Smart Investing* (Authors Choice, 2003).

The two have contributed to *Consumers Digest, Your Money,* and *Worth* magazines, as well as the *Journal of the National Association of Personal Financial Advisors, Financial Advisor,* and *Financial Planning* magazine.

Liberman's own column, "Managing Your Fortune," runs in the *Palm Beach Daily News*. She helped launch *Bank Rate Monitor* (now Bankrate.com) in North Palm Beach and was editor of the publication for 15 years. An award-winning journalist, she began her career with the Associated Press, United Press International, and United Features Syndicate. She also was a reporter for the *Courier-Post*, a Gannett newspaper in Cherry Hill, New Jersey. Liberman obtained her Bachelor's degree in journalism from Rutgers University, in New Brunswick, New Jersey. She holds a Florida real estate license and a Florida mortgage broker license.

About the Authors

Alan Lavine, author of the nation's longest-running mutual fund column, was on the ground floor of the mutual fund industry as the former director of research for IBC/Donoghue, now iMoneyNet.com, of Westborough, Massachusetts. His columns have been running in the *Boston Herald* for more than 24 years. A former Registered Investment Advisor, he also pens a regular column for the *Journal of the National Association of Personal Financial Advisors*. His articles have appeared in the *New York Times*, *Individual Investor*, *American Banker*, *Trusts and Estates*, *American Lawyer*, and *Financial World*. During the 1980s, his family finances research was cited by the Joint Economic Committee of Congress. A guest lecturer at Cornell University, Lavine has spoken before such groups as the American Psychological Association, the American Association for the Advancement of Science, the Massachusetts Psychological Association, and Morningstar, Inc.'s Mutual Fund Conference.

Lavine has a Master's degree from the University of Akron. He did post-graduate studies in finance and economics at Clark University, in Worcester, Massachusetts.

Lavine has authored *Getting Started in Mutual Funds* (Wiley, 1993); *50 Ways to Mutual Fund Profits* (McGraw-Hill, 1996); and *Your Life Insurance Options* (Wiley, 1992). He also coauthored, with Gerald Perritt, *Diversify Your Way to Wealth* (McGraw-Hill, 1993), an alternate selection of the Fortune Book Club; and *Diversify: Investors Guide to Asset-Allocation Strategies* (Longman Financial Services Publishing, 1989).

Both Liberman and Lavine are listed in Marquis's *Who's Who in America* and are members of the Society of American Business Editors and Writers.

Books by Alan Lavine and Gail Liberman

The Complete Idiot's Guide to Making Money with Mutual Funds

Rags to Retirement: Stories from People Who Retired Well on Much Less Than You'd Think!

Rags to Riches: Motivating Stories of How Ordinary People Achieved Extraordinary Wealth!

More Rages to Riches: All New Stories of How Ordinary People Achieved Extraordinary Wealth!

Love, Marriage and Money

Improving Your Credit and Reducing Your Debt

Diversify Your Way to Wealth

Short and Simple Guide to Investing

Short and Simple Guide to Life Insurance

50 Ways to Mutual Fund Profits

Getting Started in Mutual Funds

Your Life Insurance Options

Diversify: The Investors Guide to Asset Allocation Strategies

Dedication

In fondest memory of Robert K. Heady.

Acknowledgments

We'd like to thank both our present and former editors, Loretta Yates and Candace Hall, respectively, for making this book possible.

Our gratitude also goes to our development editor, Lorna Gentry.

We'd also like to thank our copy editor, Bill McManus; project editor, Tonya Simpson; and technical editor, Joe Thoma.

We Want to Hear from You!

As the reader of this book, *you* are our most important critic and commentator. We value your opinion and want to know what we're doing right, what we could do better, what areas you'd like to see us publish in, and any other words of wisdom you're willing to pass our way.

As an associate publisher for Que Publishing, I welcome your comments. You can email or write me directly to let me know what you did or didn't like about this book—as well as what we can do to make our books better.

Please note that I cannot help you with technical problems related to the topic of this book. We do have a User Services group, however, where I will forward specific technical questions related to the book.

When you write, please be sure to include this book's title and author as well as your name, email address, and phone number. I will carefully review your comments and share them with the author and editors who worked on the book.

Email: feedback@quepublishing.com

Mail: Greg Wiegand
Associate Publisher
Que Publishing
800 East 96th Street
Indianapolis, IN 46240 USA

Reader Services

Visit our website and register this book at www.quepublishing.com/register for convenient access to any updates, downloads, or errata that might be available for this book.

Introduction

Everybody wants to build wealth. Most desperately need help, which is understandable.

Lack of time is one reason few people can deal with money issues. In most households, both spouses work. There are kids, aging parents, and tons of bills to occupy any free time outside of work. With so little time to plan ahead for your financial well-being, one crisis, like car or home repairs, easily can sabotage your finances and your psyche.

Our book, *Quick Steps to Financial Stability*, aims to save you time yet help you get your financial life on track. We give you the straight scoop fast, with a very direct, step-by-step path to follow.

We also cut the time you need to manage your money by offering shortcuts to online calculators that do the hardest work for you.

We aim to keep it simple. Don't know much about money? Don't worry. We don't use the complicated jargon so often used by financial gurus. Even if you already know the ropes financially, we expect you'll find some new information in this book. That's because we both spend every workday of our lives seeking information about money.

Plus, we give you the honest, objective perspectives of experienced husband-and-wife financial authors who manage their own money. Yes, as you noticed on the cover, we have different last names, but indeed we are married. And as spouses with very different financial backgrounds and personalities, we were able to work together to achieve an important goal: to get you the information you need to improve your finances fast. Feel free to contact us at MWliblav@aol.com.

What *Quick Steps to Financial Stability* Can Do for You

So, how do you improve your financial health?

Of course, you want to know that immediately. We'll tell you. Then, we'll tell you, in simple terms, how to do it. Every chapter of *Quick Steps to Financial Stability* starts by telling you what you need to know and focuses on a simple financial management strategy. Each chapter also zeros in on the absolute simplest ways to immediately make progress toward your goals.

This book is meant for you if you

- Are not saving enough
- Feel financially stressed because your income isn't quite covering your expenses
- Are over your head in debt
- Have little time and need to learn how to manage money in the least amount of time with the best results
- Want to learn the best online websites for education, investments, insurance, and financial planning

How This Book Is Organized

The lessons and projects in this book are presented in sequence. If you work through the book from beginning to end, it'll be a snap! Yet, you easily can skip through the book to find information you need. The book is organized in three parts:

- **Part I: Are You Ready?**—You'll determine exactly where you stand financially. You'll learn how to determine your net worth and assess your income and expenses. You'll also learn how to change your attitude about money and get your family and friends on board. You'll focus on identifying all the reasons you really want money—like buying a house, having a baby, saving for your kids' higher education, and saving for your retirement. You'll also learn about health, life, disability, property and casualty, and long-term care insurance. We'll tell you how to avoid being ripped off, what insurance you truly need, and how to get professional help.

- **Part II: Creating a Simple Investment Plan**—You'll discover how to create an investment plan that works for you…fast! We'll let you know the pros and cons of investing in stocks, bonds, mutual funds, and bank accounts. We'll make it easy for you to set up a game plan that's right for you by helping you to determine what kind of investor you are. We'll give you fast ways to diversify your investments to get the best returns with as little risk as possible. We'll give you tips on how to pick investments, find information, and use simple tactics to manage your money.

- **Part III: Supercharging Your Savings Plan**—You'll learn how to put some oomph into your savings plan! We'll show you how to take advantage of special retirement tax breaks. You'll learn how to invest for retirement. You'll find quick and easy steps to save for your child's education. We'll also give you the scoop on student grants, loans, and investment plans. Plus, you'll discover how to find the best deals on loans and how to keep up your momentum. We'll tell you which aspects of your finances you need to evaluate periodically, and how often. Plus, you'll learn how to do all this while having some fun right now!

Special Elements and Icons

Throughout this book, you'll find a variety of special elements—lists, sidebars, tips, notes, cautions, graphic icons, and other extras designed to catch your eye and call out items of special interest related to the text we're discussing. We describe some of the items here. This way, as you read the book, you'll quickly spot these special elements. They're sure to help you on the path to financial stability!

To Do Lists

Each chapter of the book includes To Do Lists. The items on your To Do List give you the steps you'll need to take to complete the projects.

Special Icons

We frequently draw upon a few basic principles and time-saving tools of financial management. We've used the following icons to mark these ideas throughout the book:

Down with Debt—This icon is used to mark information and ideas that can help you cut debt. Cutting debt may be one of the most important keys to becoming financially stable.

Online Advisor—This icon marks text that can steer you to calculators that can help you figure out the task quickly. You'll also see this graphic by website addresses that have the most up-to-date information on the subject we're discussing.

Savvy Spending—This icon marks information that can help you spend your money wisely—something we definitely want you to do!

Now that you're clued in on how to spot important information, let's get going!

I

Are You Ready?

1   Examining Your Financial Condition 7

2   Identifying Your Financial Goals 23

3   Zeroing In on Your Debt 33

Examining Your Financial Condition

You go to a doctor for routine checkups, right? Now it's time for routine and (we hope) soon-to-be periodic examinations of your finances. The great news: Unlike when you go to a doctor, there's no charge for these exams. Consider this book your only co-payment.

What? You're experiencing horrible, gut-wrenching financial pain? The credit card bills are showing no mercy? The mortgage is getting tougher to pay? The price of gas is spiraling? Mother Nature has dealt you some tough blows? Unfortunately, the pharmaceutical companies haven't yet developed a pill for all these ailments. But we're on the case! Just bear with us, and we'll guide you along the path to relief.

Feeling like your finances are in great shape? Why not make them even better? We'll try to help you with this, too. Our goal is to make managing your financial life a no-lose situation, and to do it fast!

IN THIS CHAPTER:
- Analyze your net worth
- Get your income and expenses on paper
- Psych yourself up
- Mobilize family and friends!
- Free up cash

The first step is to nail down your net worth. Don't get scared. We're not asking you to sit through more classes of algebra, geometry, or trigonometry. All we want you to determine is the value of your assets, less your debts. Do you have access to a computer and the Internet and/or a calculator? If so, we'll give you quick ways to get the job done. If not, it's still not that hard. Feel free to consult with your family. We don't want you to leave anything out. The result will be the key to determining whether you are in good or bad financial shape. This won't take long—just a couple hours of your time.

When you finish this key financial checkup and take an inventory of your financial life, you can immediately take steps to change it for the better. That's what the rest of this book is about.

TO DO LIST
- ❏ Add up your assets
- ❏ Add up your liabilities
- ❏ Use those totals to calculate your net worth

Net Worth: Finding Your Bottom Line

With this chapter, we give you an immediate promotion—regardless of whether your employer or anyone else recognizes how valuable you are. We hereby promote you to the coveted position of chief executive officer (CEO) of your financial life. Don't worry—this transition is painless. Your first task is to determine your bottom line or *net worth*. After all, you need to know money-wise whether you're in the black or in the red. It is only then that you can determine whether your financial life, like any other company, needs to be turned around. Or perhaps it simply needs to be gently tweaked to generate more positive numbers. Your assets minus your liabilities equals your net worth. We can show you how to calculate your net worth, using the worksheet in Table 1.1.

WEBSITES AND PROGRAMS THAT CAN HELP

The easiest way to calculate your net worth is to visit a financial website and use its online net worth, budget, and other types of financial calculators. That way, you don't have to burden your brain adding and subtracting. Just enter the information, and voila! You get a report you can print out. You can search for online net worth calculators using Google or another search engine. Many brokerage firm, banks, insurance companies, and mutual fund companies also have excellent calculators on their websites.

Here are a few net worth calculators to consider:

- CNNMoney.com (http://cgi.money.cnn.com/tools/networth/networth.html) lets you calculate your net worth budget as easy as one, two, three.
- SmartMoney.com (www.smartmoney.com/worksheets) also has a net worth calculator.

If you prefer to work through the calculations on your own, however, grab a pencil and paper and proceed.

Step 1: Round Up Your Assets

First, working with Table 1.1 or a similar worksheet, enter or write down all your assets, which include all your money and the value of things you own. Be sure to include the values of cash in your bank accounts. Don't forget any money under your mattress. Include investments in stocks and bonds; real estate holdings; ownership in a private business; retirement savings accounts such as IRAs, 401(k)s, SIMPLE plans, SEPs, Keoghs, or pension plans; annuities; the cash value of your life insurance; and the value of your car, home, jewelry, and other property. If you have your own business, evaluating it is a complex accounting task. Your accountant looks at the "net present value," a calculation based on your business assets, liabilities, ongoing expenses, historical revenues, and estimated revenues. But to keep things simple for this exercise, why not simply call a business broker and ask what similar businesses have sold for in your area?

Table 1.1 Determine Your Assets

Asset	Value
Checking account(s)	$
Other bank savings accounts	$
Mutual funds, stocks, and bonds	$

Table 1.1 Continued

Asset	Value
Real estate other than home	$
Private business	$
Life insurance cash value	$
Retirement accounts	$
Annuities	$
Your home	$
Auto(s)	$
Jewelry	$
Other personal property	$
Total Assets	$

Step 2: List All Your Liabilities or Debts

Liabilities include credit card debt, car loans, student loans, mortgages, income taxes, life insurance policy loans, and any other loans. Use Table 1.2 or a similar worksheet to list your liabilities.

Table 1.2 Determine Your Liabilities

Liability	Amount Owed
Credit card debt	$
Other charge card debt	$
Income taxes payable	$
Bank loan(s)	$
Insurance policy loan(s)	$
Car loan(s)	$
Student loan(s)	$
Home mortgage	$
Mortgage on other property	$
Home equity loan(s)	$

Table 1.2 Continued

Liability	Amount Owed
Brokerage account loan(s)	$
Other loans	$
Total Liabilities	$

Step 3: Subtract Your Liabilities from Your Assets

Subtract the value of the "Total Liabilities" line in Table 1.2 from the "Total Assets" line in Table 1.1. Is the result positive or negative? If it's positive, you have a positive net worth. If it's negative, you have a negative net worth. But even if it's negative, don't worry. Help is on the way! By realizing exactly how much you're under water, you've successfully mastered the first step toward getting your financial life afloat.

> **NOTE** The net worth of the median American household was $93,100 in 2004, according to the Federal Reserve. That includes real estate assets and retirement accounts. The average savings rate of Americans is approaching −2%. Where do you stand?

TO DO LIST

- ❏ Determine your monthly income
- ❏ Categorize your monthly expenses
- ❏ Discover where your money goes each month
- ❏ Set new targets for your expenses and income

Reviewing Income and Expenses

As the first step toward gaining control of your finances, you need to understand exactly what money is coming in every month and where that money is going. Then, you need to set money targets as to how much less you'd like to spend and how much more you'd like to earn.

We hate to use the term *budget*, so we won't. Let's just call this an exercise. This exercise won't cause you to lose pounds and inches around your waist, but it will help you lose a little financial weight. Its aim: to find extra cash you never realized you had and, perhaps, bring in some new cash. Much like when you're counting calories, this becomes much easier once you know the hard numbers. Armed with facts, you'll be able to zero in on the best ways to cut spending and/or increase income. Then, you'll be able to put a lot more money to work for you.

> **TIP** Want to save time? The following are links to some personal finance calculators that can help you do the work:
>
> www.finance.cch.com/tools/calcs.asp. In the Personal Finance category, click on Home Budget Analyzer. Click on Expenses Calc and Paycheck Calc and enter figures.
>
> http://cgi.money.cnn.com/tools/. Click on Ideal Budget in the Debt category.

Step 1: Calculate Your Monthly Income

To begin, use Table 1.3 to determine exactly how much money you have coming in each month. Start by entering all sources of monthly income, by category, as shown in the table. Then add monthly figures in each category so that you also have the annual figures.

> **TIP** The "deposit" section of your checkbook register can be a great help with the task of categorizing your monthly income. Paycheck stubs, bank statements, and investment statements also help.

Include take-home pay of all contributing family members and any income that may come from investments, such as rents, or alimony and Social Security. Don't forget monthly income you might be getting from IRAs or other retirement plans, pension plans, and interest on your savings.

Table 1.3 Income Worksheet

Income	Monthly	Target	Yearly	Target
Wages	$			
Investment income	$			
Bank account income	$			
Rental income	$			
Alimony	$			

Table 1.3 Continued

Income	Monthly	Target	Yearly	Target
Social Security	$			
Other income	$			
Total Income	**$**			

Step 2: Categorize Monthly Expenses

Next, use Table 1.4 to enter all monthly expenses by category. Include rent or mortgage, taxes, utilities, household maintenance (such as cleaning service, exterminator, lawn service, and so forth), and other expenses. Total your grocery bills, restaurant bills, and non-food expenses. Add your auto expenses—car payments, fuel bills, repairs, licenses, parking, tolls, gas, and other related expenses. Include all your insurance costs and your vacation and entertainment expenses. Then, list your other expenses like child care, child support or alimony, gifts, educational expenses, hobbies, dues, newspaper and magazine subscriptions, pets, allowances, and other miscellaneous expenses. Whew! Why is it that our financial lives always seem to include so many more categories of expenses than income?

You're almost done!

Table 1.4 Expenses Worksheet

Income	Monthly	Target	Yearly	Target
Rent	$			
Mortgage	$			
Utilities				
Electric, gas, water, garbage, sewer	$			
Telephone, cable TV, Internet service	$			
Food	$			
Clothing	$			
Personal care	$			
Auto Repairs	$			
Gas	$			
Other auto expenses	$			

Table 1.4 Continued

Income	Monthly	Target	Yearly	Target
Doctor	$			
Dental	$			
Eye care	$			
Drugs	$			
Other Medical expenses	$			
Auto insurance	$			
Health insurance	$			
Homeowners insurance	$			
Life insurance	$			
Disability insurance	$			
Other insurance	$			
Vacation and travel	$			
Dining out	$			
Other entertainment	$			
Child care	$			
Child support	$			
Donations	$			
Education	$			
Hobbies	$			
Dues	$			
Newspapers, books, subscriptions	$			
Pets	$			
Allowances	$			
Bank investments	$			
Mutual funds investments	$			
Brokerage investments	$			
IRA or pension investments	$			
Miscellaneous expenses	$			
Total Expenses	$			

Step 3: Determine Where You Stand

The next step is to find out how much money you have left over after you meet expenses. Total all your monthly expenses and annual expenses from the "Total Expenses" lines in Table 1.4. Subtract those amounts from your corresponding monthly and annual income figures. Positive numbers mean you're in the black. Negative numbers mean you're in the red. Now that you finally know where you stand, you can start setting some new targets. Onward and upward!

> **TIP** Microsoft Money and Intuit Quicken Premier are excellent software packages you can use to develop your own financial plan.

CHANGING YOUR ATTITUDES ABOUT MONEY

How would you like to have as much money as Microsoft's Bill Gates? What about renown investor and businessman Warren Buffett? Talk show hostess Oprah Winfrey? Entertainment giants Gloria and Emilio Estefan? Impossible, you say? Well, maybe we're reaching a tad high. But we can point to a number of people who started from nothing and managed to build a net worth of at least $1 million. Just read our other best-selling book, *Rags to Riches*. We even found more examples for our sequel, *More Rags to Riches*. It's definitely not out of the realm of possibilities. One trait we observed during our interviews: Many successful people stopped believing they couldn't be successful. They refused to believe that the rich were another breed or any different from them. They shunned lotteries, with their extremely unfavorable odds. They ignored the negative feedback of teachers and friends. They read a lot or attended seminars. They figured out what they enjoyed doing, set objectives with that in mind, and took advantage of opportunities to reach those goals. Even if you haven't quite managed to develop a Microsoft Windows program and you have a lousy voice and television presence, there's hope. The trick is to take hold of the reins on your financial life, regardless of what you do for a living. Do you have a negative net worth that you'd like to reverse? Go for it! Would you like to live a more luxurious life than you currently have? Let's make it happen!

Setting Your Financial Goals

Like any company, you and your family members need to develop your overall financial goals. This process is definitely a family affair. (No family or significant others involved with your financial affairs? In that case, you're on your own.) The objectives of other people involved with your financial life, however, may not always be the same as yours. Dealing with others can prove one of the most difficult tasks when it comes to managing your money. Do you have a spouse who likes to buy all the latest fashions? Did you have to pull out the credit card to get Junior his Xbox 360 last holiday season? If so, these situations can become major obstacles in your effort to improve the bottom line of your financial life.

That's why we'd like you, at this stage, to round up all family members or parties directly involved with your financial life for a board of directors meeting. Set a time and place that's convenient for all to get together. Prepare a written agenda, and bring all your hard information to the meeting, including the worksheets you developed showing your net worth, income, and expenses. These will be the focus of your meeting.

First, examine your net worth worksheet. Is it negative? In that case, your goal might be to set it on a positive track. If you have savings, but need $10,000 for Junior's college education, say so. Obtain a commitment of support from the members of your team. We'll talk more about fine-tuning your goals in Chapter 2, "Identifying Your Financial Goals."

The ball for determining your financial goals strictly lies in your court.

TO DO LIST

- ❏ Explore ways to lower debt
- ❏ Take simple steps to trim expenses
- ❏ Find ways to bring in more money

Freeing Up Quick Cash

If your expenses are exceeding income, you need to first determine why. Brainstorm what you can do to change the situation.

Forget the idea of buying more lottery tickets! Dressing the part won't necessarily improve your situation either. Nor will buying a fancy car. Rather, you can start on the road to good money management—whether with your family or alone—by looking at each line of your income and expenses worksheet with a sharp pencil in hand. The objective: You need to get your income substantially higher than expenses.

Controlling Your Debt

One major key to controlling your debt—as you no doubt have heard before—is to stop paying interest on all loans. Revolving interest can be a money management killer.

This might be easier said than done! But if your net worth needs a major turnaround, we urge you to start by taking the credit cards out of your wallet. This immediately will stop you from accumulating more debt by charging purchases on impulse. Yes, credit cards generate impulse spending—exactly what you're probably trying to avoid. It's true. Why do you think major retail stores all issue credit cards? Credit card promoters have them convinced that you'll spend some 24% to nearly 70% more per purchase in their stores. We've seen the sales literature. Do you really need to be letting all that extra dough fly out of your financial life?

Trimming Expenses

Only you and (if applicable) your spouse and/or family can determine how best to improve your bottom line. Every situation is different. But as an example, here are some general guidelines we calculated, based on the Bureau of Labor Statistics Consumer Expenditures Survey, released in 2005, about what percentage of our income before taxes we spend for daily living:

- 21% on food both at home (10%) and away from home (11%)
- 32% on housing
- 4% on clothing
- 18% on transportation
- 6% on health care
- 5% on entertainment
- 14% on other expenses such as medical, utilities, installment debt, and life insurance

> **TIP** To get a more precise estimate of what you should be spending for a family of your size and in your geographic neighborhood, visit the Economic Policy Institute (www.epi.org). Under Web Features, click on Online Calculators. Then click Basic Family Budget Calculator. Enter your family type and the state and city in which you reside and click Submit. The calculator will tell you how much it should cost you to live in that area.

How much are you spending? If your family is spending substantially more than some of the measures we just gave you, perhaps you can figure out ways to cut. Might you consider downsizing to a smaller or less expensive home? Can you shop at less expensive clothing stores? Might you consider increasing your health insurance deductible to lower your monthly cost?

Any spending you can cut in these areas can be rerouted toward paying off your debt and then opening a bank account or investment account. Go to Chapter 3, "Zeroing In on Your Debt," for more details on dealing with your debt. If you have no debt, consider ways that you might boost your earnings. Whatever savings you can muster in this exercise can go directly toward building a financially healthy life for you and your family.

Here are a few more painless ideas to help cut spending:

- Buy brand name goods at discount factory outlets. Wait for sales at your favorite store.
- Do more haggling. People have always negotiated the price of their autos. Try it with that new washing machine, refrigerator, or air conditioner.
- Clip coupons when you go grocery shopping. But beware. Coupons often are for brand names, which may be more expensive than generic brands—even with the coupons.
- Avoid long-distance phone calls. Wait for your friends to call you. Or consider using a cell phone that gives you a free number of hours for local and long distance calls. When possible, communicate long distance by e-mail rather than by telephone.
- Increase insurance deductibles. You can save a few hundred dollars a year by increasing the deductibles on your auto, homeowners, health, and dental insurance. Why pay the insurance company higher premiums when you might not use the services as much as you think?
- Take your lunch to work. At today's whopping prices, you can immediately save as much as $200 per month.
- Stop smoking and avoid chewing gum. Cut out any other costly, unhealthy habits.
- Before you grocery shop, make a list. Shop only on a full stomach to ward off impulse buying. Check cabinets first to see what you already have on hand. Check ads for sale items. Consider replacing expensive meats and cold cuts with cheaper pastas, chicken, rice, and veggies. Plan meals ahead, and hang on to leftovers.

- Cut down on more expensive paper products or buy them in bulk.
- Invite friends over rather than going out to dinner. If you do go out, consider drinking your wine before you leave. Avoid the added expense of coffee.
- Instead of drinking costly soda and coffee at work, switch to free water.
- Use your public library for publications and DVD rentals. Cut costly magazine subscriptions and movie rentals.
- Take vacations closer to home and during the off season when rates are cheaper.
- Cut financial services expenses. Look for banks with the lowest fees. Search around for free checking and no-fee credit cards. Great sources include www.bankrate.com; www.hsh.com; www.cardweb.com; and www.imoneynet.com.
- Switch to energy-efficient light bulbs and use water savers on your faucets and sprinkler systems. Use native plants that require no extra water in your landscape. Plant shade trees.
- Shop for generic prescription drugs and generic food brands.
- Sell a second car if you don't use it much. You'll save on insurance, repairs, and monthly car payments. You still can rent a car when you need it for some $20 to $40 per day. Before shelling out money for insurance on a rental car, check to see if your credit card and/or auto insurance policy provides coverage.
- Check the equity in your home. If it's more than 20%, contact your lender and see if you can eliminate costly mortgage insurance.
- Save old cell phones. You can use them free for emergency phone calls.
- Avoid telephone answering services if possible and save monthly fees. Buy an inexpensive, reliable machine.

If you're ready to make more substantial changes in the pursuit of lowering your expenses, you might explore these options:

- Move to a lower-cost region. Cost of living comparisons are available at http://cgi.money.cnn.com/tools/costofliving/costofliving.html; www.homefair.com (click on The

> **NOTE** We urge you and your family to come up with your own creative ways to cut spending and free up more cash. In fact, if you have any good ones, please e-mail us at MWliblav@aol.com. We never can get enough ideas of painless ways to save money!

Salary Calculator). Also, check in your public library. Some magazines, including *Money* and *Forbes*, regularly publish lists of the best places to live. Information also is at www.realestatejournal.com.

- Downsize to a smaller or less expensive home or condo.

Beefing Up Your Income

Of course, the flip side of the coin is to increase your income. There are some fast fixes for that also, so we urge you to be sure to add some targets in the Income column of the income and expenses worksheet. Here are just a few to consider:

- Ask your employer for a hard-earned raise. Visit www.careerjournal.com to document average wages for your line of work. Gather hard numbers to present to your employer.
- Research which employers in your area pay the most and seek a higher-paying job.
- Take on an additional part-time job. Consider babysitting or delivering newspapers.
- Rent out a room of your home or get a roommate.
- Buy a home and rent your existing home for a positive cash flow, if possible.
- Clean out your attic and hold a garage sale.
- Consider earning extra income as a mystery shopper. Visit the Mystery Shoppers Providers Association at www.mysteryshop.org to find available assignments in your area. Beware, however, of answering blind newspaper ads for mystery shoppers. Many have been scams.

> **TIP** The Bureau of Labor Statistics publishes information about jobs, opportunities, and salaries at its website, www.bls.gov. In its latest 2000 survey, airplane pilots and navigators were the highest-paid full-time workers, averaging $95.80 an hour. Physicians were next, earning $61.19 an hour. By contrast, registered nurses average $21.69 an hour and maids $7.87 an hour.

> **TIP** We've read repeatedly that Costco tends to pay above-average wages and benefits to its employees.

- Make certain you're getting all the tax breaks possible. Military combat personnel, who aren't filing federal income tax returns, for example, may be missing out on the valuable Earned Income Tax Credit. The tax credit, which means you get money back, is for certain people who work and have limited earned income. Visit www.irs.gov for more information.
- Check out the IRS withholding calculator at www.irs.gov to determine whether you might increase your income by taking fewer deductions on IRS Form W-4.

TRACKING DOWN BENEFITS YOU DESERVE

Determine whether you're collecting all possible benefits to which you're entitled. Find out about Social Security, supplemental security benefits, and disability at www.ssa.gov. Learn about housing assistance at www.hud.gov and veterans' benefits at www.va.gov. Persons with low income should telephone electric and phone companies to learn about special programs offering discounts or free service. Find out about food stamps and welfare at www.cms.hhs.gov. Contact religious organizations and local, state, and federal housing authorities. Referral services for financial aid may include your area agency on aging. Visit www.n4a.org. Also, in many areas you might be able to call 211 to obtain emergency assistance.

- Put all change that threatens to burst your wallet into a large container. Periodically deposit it.
- Search www.missingmoney.com to see if you inadvertently left behind any assets anywhere—perhaps in safe deposit boxes, forgotten financial accounts, or with previous employers. This website, sponsored by the National Association of Unclaimed Property Administrators, helps owners recover lost assets legally required to revert to participating states. Great news! While researching this book, we found assets belonging to at least one family member!

Summary

We hope that in this chapter we've succeeded in getting you to eliminate the emotions behind your financial condition—good or bad. To effectively manage your money, you must take a hard, objective look at your bottom line or net worth, and the money going in and out of your life—in other words, your income and expenses. Once you can nail down where the money is coming from and where it is going, you can determine what steps you can take to get more money in and less money out! Two ways to get started: cut expenses and/or increase income. In Chapter 2, we'll have you determine exactly what you want and how much you'll need on the road to financial stability.

2

Identifying Your Financial Goals

Preparing for Life

Now that you've analyzed your financial state of affairs, the next step is to make sure you have the proper insurance and legal documents. In this chapter, you'll find a helpful checklist to ensure that you don't forget anything. Right now, concentrate on planning for the future. The sooner you start, the better.

You're already on the right path to saving money rather than spending everything. This chapter is the fun part. Grab a pencil and paper and list all the important things you'd like to have over the next several years.

Your short-term savings goals may include saving for a vacation, new furniture, home improvements, a new washer and dryer set, a refrigerator, a TV, or a computer. Longer-term goals might be saving for a baby, retirement, your child's college education, or a wedding.

IN THIS CHAPTER:

- Prepare for life's most common costs
- Plan for buying a home and achieving other big financial goals

TO DO LIST

- ❏ Determine what you have and what you need in the way of insurance and protective legal documents
- ❏ Set your financial goals
- ❏ Evaluate the best ways to save

Identifying Your Insurance Needs

As we once heard Donald Trump say "Protect the downside and the rest takes care of itself." For this, unfortunately, you need insurance and some protective legal documents.

Determine what insurance protection you have and what you still need. You probably already know you need to have health insurance, in case you're hospitalized, and life insurance to protect your family when you're not around. But there's more. Use the following checklist to determine how protected you and your family really are.

If there are any gaps, we'll help you close them. In Chapter 6, "Protecting the Downside: Insurance and Other Safeguards," we'll give you a lot more detail about insurance and the legal documents you might want to consider.

Downside Preparedness Checklist

Health insurance _____

Disability insurance _____

Long-term care insurance _____

Life insurance _____

Homeowners or rental insurance _____

Auto insurance _____

Will _____

Power of attorney _____

Healthcare power of attorney or surrogate _____

Guardianship papers for your children _____

Setting Financial Goals

Back to your goals.

The first goal automatically should be an emergency savings fund designed to cover six months' worth of living expenses. Make sure it's enough to cover any emergencies—like a job loss, car repair, medical or dental expense, or natural disaster. This way, you won't have to tap those high-cost credit cards! Plus, if you have any investments, you won't be forced to cash them out when they're down in value. Other goals might include saving for major purchases and expenses, such as buying a car or funding your child's education.

Draw up a list of all your financial goals, and indicate on that list when you want to achieve each goal and what it will cost. Table 2.1 shows an example of how your list of goals should look.

Table 2.1 Sample Financial Goals List

Item Desired	When (Years to Save)	What It Costs
Emergency fund	3 years	$15,000
An LCD TV	1 year	$1,000
Living room furniture	1 1/2 to 2 years	$3,000
Car down payment	3 years	$2,200
A dream vacation	4 years	$2,500
Down payment on a house	5 years	$20,000
Child's college	18 years	$50,000
Child's wedding	22 years	$10,000
Down payment on second home	15 years	$25,000
Retirement	30 years	$612,500

Use an online search engine, such as Google, to help you nail down costs. Online calculators that also can help calculate costs are available at the following websites:

- www.collegeboard.com (click Pay for College after initially entering the site as either a parent or a student)
- www.practicalmoneyskills.com

Websites with calculators that can help you manage your goals and determine how much you'll need to save each month to reach each goal include the following:

- http://alaskaadvantage.state.ak.us/calc/savings.html
- www.choosetosave.org
- www.bankrate.com
- www.myfico.com
- www.finance.cch.com

Don't have access to a computer? No problem. Just turn to old-fashioned pencil and paper.

> **TIP** There's more to life than just spending and saving money. You have to enjoy the good things life has to offer. You'll want to reward yourself with some fun weekend getaways, a dream vacation, an LCD or plasma TV, or even, if you so decide, that new sports car. Be sure to add those to your goals list too.

Considering Your Savings Plan

The most important thing to remember in this chapter: The longer you have to save, the less painful it will be, and the more bang you'll get for the buck.

Assume you can earn a 4% rate of return. Here's how much you must save monthly to have $1,000, rounded up to the nearest dollar, within the specified period:

- 1 year: $82
- 2 years: $41
- 3 years: $27
- 4 years: $20
- 5 years: $16
- 6 years: $12
- 7 years: $11
- 8 years: $9
- 9 years: $8
- 10 years: $7

> **NOTE** Avoiding credit cards can be one way to spend about one-third less. If you pay cash for everything, you think much harder about what you buy.
>
> Don't want to give up plastic because you get cash, airline miles, or points toward merchandise for using your card? Don't buy into these marketing ploys too heavily. As you learned in Chapter 1, "Examining Your Financial Condition," these incentives are designed to accelerate impulse spending, which, if you're not careful, can keep you from achieving your goals. You also may build debt by racking up interest and fees. On the other hand, if you can strictly control what you buy, and your credit card offers you rewards you can use, who are we to stop you from getting something for nothing?

Where will all this money come from, you ask? We already gave you some ideas in Chapter 1. We challenge you to come up with some more ideas on your own. One fast fix we especially like is bringing your lunch to work. That's at least an extra $150 to $300 monthly that you can save, if both working spouses do this. Cut out any services you truly don't need, such as extra cable channels or call waiting, and consider some romantic dinners at home rather than in restaurants. You're already on the way!

Consider calling all your previous employers to make certain there are no pensions, health benefits, or profit-sharing plans you might have left behind.

There also may be ways to scale down your goals. For example, wait two years to buy that LCD TV, and we're willing to wager you'll be able to get it for much less than its current price. Then, you'll be able to use the money you saved to meet some of your other goals. You might also consider some dream vacation destinations a bit closer to home to shave the cost.

Once you've mustered up more added cash, technology is on your side. Simply arrange with your bank or investment company to automatically have the amount you're saving deducted from your checking account and invested. Do this before you pay any bills, and before you have a chance to spend it anyplace else. You won't even notice that money is gone.

First route this automatic payment to a bank savings account.

Say you invest your entire newfound cash—$150 per month or $1,800 per year—at a bank savings rate of 4%: in 10 years, you would have almost $22,100. That money can go a long way toward longer-term goals. Imagine if you can find even more cash to invest or obtain an even higher return! We'll give you ideas on how to do that later in the book.

We chose a 4% return as a relatively conservative estimate. Squeeze out a return of 5% or 6%, and your money goes even further.

> **CAUTION** If you're saving for less than five years, play it safe. Invest only in federally insured bank accounts or U.S. Treasury notes that mature in five years or less. Have more than five years to invest? In that case, you might consider riskier investments, such as stocks or bonds. We provide more details about this in Chapter 4, "Weighing the Pros and Cons of Simple Investment Options," and Chapter 5, "Creating a Plan That Works for You."

> **NOTE** Don't be discouraged at the high monthly totals for your financial goals. Remember that your kids might qualify for educational financial aid, and that you get Social Security and Medicare in retirement.

After you've accumulated enough money to reach one goal, continue saving the same amount. Just route it to another goal on your list. The speed at which you reach your objectives will be compounded. Add in any pay raises, and you're well on your way to great money management fast!

TO DO LIST

- ❏ Plan for buying a home
- ❏ Plan for having a baby
- ❏ Estimate the cost of a college education and retirement

Planning for Big Goals

There are a few big goals you definitely want to consider. Naturally, achieving big financial goals requires more thought and effort, so we discuss them in a little more depth.

Buying a Home

Reaching your financial goals can get much easier if you buy a home wisely. Reason: Ultimately, when you pay off your mortgage, you'll no longer have to pay big bucks for a place to live. You can route that added savings toward reaching your other financial goals and improving your lifestyle.

Also, many who itemize deductions on their 1040 income tax form claim a deduction on home mortgage interest paid. You also may deduct real estate taxes. This can put more income in your pocket while you're living there. Because of these deductions, you ultimately may be able to live in a nicer home for less money than you'd pay to rent a lower-quality house.

In addition, you get to keep the profits you make once you sell the house, which ultimately can boost your net worth—a major objective of this book. Unlike most other investments, you pay no capital gains tax on the sale of a home, provided that you meet two conditions:

- You've lived in your home for at least two of the prior five years.
- Your capital gains—or profits from the sale of your home, less money you put into it—are not more than $250,000, $500,000 per couple.

CAN YOU AFFORD A HOME?

The median price of a home as we wrote this chapter was running over $200,000. Don't forget to throw in maintenance, insurance, and property taxes. To see if you can afford a home, with a mortgage, why not do the calculations that lenders do—before you get in over your head?

Lenders often look at two ratios:

Housing ratio. This is your monthly housing expenses as a percentage of your gross monthly income. Simply add up all the money you'd be spending monthly on a home. This includes

- Mortgage payment
- Monthly taxes
- Monthly hazard insurance
- Monthly condo or homeowner fees

Divide the sum by your gross monthly income (your income before taxes are taken out). Lenders typically like the result to be about 28% or less.

Debt ratio, or total obligation ratio, is the percentage of your monthly gross income that you can spend on both housing and long-term debt (debt you'll be paying at least 10 months). For this, add

- Your monthly housing payment
- Car loans
- Student loans
- Credit cards
- Other loans or bills

Divide the sum by your gross monthly income. Lenders like this result to be within about 36% of your gross monthly income.

If you're a little off on those ratios, don't despair. They're definitely not engraved in stone. You still might qualify for a local, state, or federal mortgage program that is more lenient.

In addition, lenders also consider your credit reports. The most important thing they want to know is that you have a history of paying on time (more about this in Chapter 3, "Zeroing In on Your Debt").

Online Advisor

A number of online calculators can help you determine not only how much of a home you can afford, but also whether you should rent or own a home. The following websites, among others, offer such calculators:

- www.hsh.com
- www.yahoo.com (click on Real Estate, click on the Home Loans tab, and then click Calculators)
- www.realtor.com (click on Home Finance)
- www.mortgageunderwriters.com
- www.ginniemae.gov

If you decide to add buying a home to your list of goals, be sure to include the down payment and any mortgage closing costs.

Having a Baby

Want to have a family? Expect to shell out some $9,000 in the child's first year alone. Meanwhile, you'll spend another $134,000 to $270,000 to raise a child from birth through age 17, according to the U.S. Department of Agriculture. The good news is that Uncle Sam grants you a dependent deduction and, possibly, a child tax credit, on your federal income taxes. You also might be able to write off some medical, dental, educational, and other expenses. So be sure to consult your accountant and visit www.irs.gov for more information.

> **TIP** Still on the fence about buying a home? Consider visiting a housing counselor, who can walk you through your decision. You can find housing counselors in your area, approved by the U.S. Department of Housing and Urban Development, at www.hud.gov or by calling 800-569-4287.

Please don't let the high price tag of parenthood mar this otherwise happy event. Logistically and financially, it just requires some planning to get you further ahead than many families. Use Table 2.2 to help estimate your baby's cost in the first year alone. You might ask your doctor's office for the cost of the doctor and hospital. Contact your attorney and insurance agent for estimated added insurance and legal costs. Search other costs individually online or when you go shopping, and multiply individual items, such as diapers, by the number of times you'll likely need to purchase them in the first year.

Table 2.2 New Baby Cost Checklist

Item	Cost
Hospital:	
Hospital bills	$
Doctor bills	$
Baby:	
Clothes	$
Blankets	$
Disposable diapers	$
Booties and socks	$
Nursery:	
Sheets	$
Waterproof pads	$
Blankets	$
Crib and mattress	$
Bassinet	$
Portable baby seat	$
Baby carriage	$
Feeding equipment	$
Bath items	$
Miscellaneous	$
Additional considerations:	
Increase life insurance	$
Add child to your health insurance	$
Purchase or increase disability insurance	$
Revise your wills	$
Appoint guardians for your child	$
Total Cost	$

Add up all the money you think you'll need to have a baby and include that in your goals.

Saving for Your Children's Education and Retirement

These may be two of your largest goals. The good news is that there's a lot of assistance out there to help you reach them. So much so, that we've devoted entire chapters to each of these objectives. You'll find the information you need in Chapter 7, "Saving for Retirement," and Chapter 8, "How to Pay for Your Children's Education." In the meantime, use these benchmarks to help finalize your important list of goals.

The College Board reported that for the 2005-2006 school year, one year of a private college costs an average of $29,026—that's including tuition, fees, and room and board. Multiply that times four and you're talking close to $120,000 for a four-year school—assuming your child wants to live in a dorm. A public institution costs $12,127, including tuition, fees, and room and board. That's $48,000 to live away from home for four years. By contrast, your child can go to a two-year public college for an average of $2,191, or a little over $4,000, for the full two years. The added costs of room and board likely won't be necessary.

As for your retirement, the rule of thumb is that you'll need 70% of your current salary. So calculate that figure, and use it to compute your goal of retiring. Don't feel like doing all that work? Just use the following benchmark for now. Adjust it upward or downward, based on your current salary. Say you're making $35,000 annually. In that case, you'd want at least $24,500 annually to live on, based upon your need to retain 70% of that in your golden years. Assuming you earn an annual interest rate of just 4%, you'd need a stash of $612,500. Seem impossible? Please don't despair. You're apt to have a little help from, at the very least, Uncle Sam. Plus, you're already on your way to becoming a great manager of your financial life.

Summary

In this chapter, you determined exactly what you need to do to protect the downside of your financial life as well as reasons you truly want to save money. You also calculated the cost of these desires. Consider posting on your refrigerator or some other conspicuous spot the list of financial goals you've developed in this chapter. Check it out each time before you go shopping. You'll think longer and harder before you spend your money on things that really won't help you meet these objectives. Be sure to have any extra money you can save automatically deducted—initially into a savings account. Then watch your financial life take a sharp turn for the better!

In Chapter 3, we'll tell you how to deal with any debt that could derail your efforts.

3

Zeroing In on Your Debt

IN THIS CHAPTER:
- Quickly cut your debt
- Know your rights with debt
- Improve your credit score

On the path to a great financial life, it's easy to get sidetracked by debt. This chapter gives you strategies to improve your creditworthiness and cut your debt.

The first part of the chapter focuses on ways to pay off those darn credit cards and other loans. The last part tackles the credit score that lenders use to measure your credit risk.

Your credit score is a statistic that is considered by an increasing array of financial service providers when they issue you credit. Your credit score also could have a dramatic impact on the price you pay for credit.

In this chapter, we give you the straight scoop on dealing with debt, and tell you how to get your credit score as high as possible. A high credit score means you have a great track record in paying off debt. Complete the tasks given in this chapter and you'll be that much closer to reaching your financial goals!

TO DO LIST

- [ ] Determine whether you have a debt problem
- [ ] Choose an option for dealing with your debt
- [ ] Understand your credit score
- [ ] Take steps to get your credit score as high as possible

Over Your Head in Debt? Try These Fixes

The first step is to nail down whether you already have a debt problem. Take this short test to determine whether you're in financial hot water:

1. Is more than 20% of your take-home pay used for credit card payments, excluding the mortgage?
2. Is the balance in your savings account shrinking?
3. Are your credit card balances growing even though you're making monthly payments?
4. Are you close to hitting your credit card borrowing limits?
5. Are you making just minimum payments on your credit cards?
6. Do you have a hard time paying your rent or mortgage?
7. Have you gotten calls because you're late paying the bills?
8. Are you using a cash advance on one credit card to pay off another?

If you answered yes to any of these questions, your financial life may be headed for trouble. Exactly how serious is your problem? That depends. But, if you're having difficulty meeting your monthly obligations, you have some options, as discussed in the next section.

> **TIP** Already being hounded by debt collectors? You have some rights under the Fair Debt Collection Practices Act, which you can read more about at www.ftc.gov. For personal, family, and household debts, you can stop debt collectors from contacting you simply by writing letters and asking them to stop. Upon receiving your letter, a collector may only contact you again to say that there will be no further contact, or that the creditor intends to take a specific action. Even if calls stop, however, you still could be sued for the debt.

CHAPTER 3   Zeroing In on Your Debt   35

TO DO LIST

- ❏ Control your debt
- ❏ Understand the pros and cons of credit counseling
- ❏ Consolidate your debt
- ❏ Learn about the bankruptcy option

Controlling Debt Yourself

If your debt problem is not totally out of control, why not handle it yourself?

It never hurts to ask lenders to lower your interest rates. Interest rates typically are not reported to credit bureaus. Some lenders may lower the rate to keep your business.

Many lenders also may agree to modify other terms of your loan agreement, such as the monthly payment, if you're having serious problems and contact them. But beware that a modified payment could be noted on your credit report. This could lower your credit score quite a bit.

If you have a lot of debt but believe you ultimately can repay it, we urge you to revisit your income and expense worksheet in Chapter 1, "Examining Your Financial Condition." Be sure to set monthly targets for your income and expenses. Each month, review how close you are to meeting the amounts you have targeted in each category. Then figure out what more you can do to cut expenses or increase income enough to get there. In addition, you must stop using those credit cards.

> **CAUTION** Standard on many credit card agreements now is a "universal default clause." This means that a lower credit score due to a single loan or credit card problem could automatically trigger higher rates on your other credit cards. Also, when lenders modify your payment, you actually may owe more interest. This could happen if you're paying your balance off over a longer period.

To self-control your debt, take this action:

1. Cut up your credit cards, or put them in a drawer and stop using them.
2. Free up as much money as possible through some of the tactics we told you about in Chapter 1. Take at least $50 to $100 per month—more, if possible—and route it toward increasing your monthly credit card or loan

payments. Pay off your highest interest rate credit card or loan first. Or, if it seems easier, start on the card with the lowest balance. Once you've paid off one card, double up on your monthly payments on another card or loan.

Here's a simple example of how this tactic works. Assume you have a credit card balance of $5,000 at 12% interest. Cut your expenses enough to pay $200 monthly toward that balance. You'd pay off your credit card in two years and five months.

3. Once you're debt-free, you're all set to start saving toward your financial goals. Assume you reroute that $200 monthly payment toward savings at a 6% annual rate. In 10 years, you will have saved $32,776 toward your financial goals.

> **CAUTION** Don't close unused credit card accounts and, if possible, avoid shifting balances to another account. Having fewer open accounts may lower your credit score.

> **TIP** Did you find a lot more cash while evaluating your income and expenses? Consider routing one-half of your newfound money toward paying off the highest-rate credit card or loan. Put the other half toward saving for your financial goals. This way, you'll also have some savings to tap in an emergency, and can keep those credit cards filed away!

Credit Counseling

If you're uncertain about how serious your debt situation is, consider obtaining credit counseling from a nonprofit agency.

Following are the primary national networks of agencies that provide counseling:

- The National Foundation for Credit Counseling, Silver Spring, Maryland, www.nfcc.org. Phone: 800-388-2227.
- The Association of Independent Consumer Credit Counseling Agencies (AICCCA), Fairfax, Virginia, www.aiccca.org. Phone: 800-450-1794.

> **CAUTION** Lenders warn that a contact with a credit counseling service could result in a notation on your credit report, even though it is not factored into your credit score. Down the road, this notation could hurt your chances of qualifying for a loan. So before meeting with any debt counselor, try to confirm that your initial counseling session won't be reported to a consumer reporting agency or credit bureau.

Often, credit counseling agencies, which are funded, at least in part, by lenders, will help you develop a debt repayment plan. They'll likely require you to make your monthly payments to them and may charge a fee up front and/or in the payment. If you sign onto a debt management plan, always get a written agreement that includes the price, services to be performed, how long it will take to complete the plan, and the company's business name and address. Call your creditors and confirm the counseling organization is making payments on time. For more information on selecting a debt counselor, see Appendix B, "Finding the Right Help."

> **NOTE** Be aware that you must see a government-approved credit counseling agency within six months before you file bankruptcy. To make sure the agency you see is government approved, view that list at www.usdoj.gov/ust.

Consolidating Your Debts

Should you consolidate all your debts—roll everything you owe into one big loan? There are pluses and minuses to loan consolidation.

You might be able to save money by consolidating your debts and lowering your loan payments. For example, say you owe $5,000 at 18% interest and want to pay off the debt in three years. Refinance that debt at 9% over the same period, and you'll save $783 in interest and cut your monthly payments $22, from $181 to $159.

There are other ways to consolidate your loans. One example is to get a lower-rate credit card, which many banks are aggressively promoting. So if you qualify, you might consider rolling the high-rate debt to a lower-rate card. The drawbacks:

- Credit card loan interest isn't tax-deductible.
- Many credit cards charge variable rates, so if interest rates rise, your low-rate credit card soon could become high-rate.
- Shifting balances from one credit card to another could cause a dip in your credit score.
- Many of the low-rate offers are teaser rates, riddled with fees and/or high rates for any missteps, such as a late payment or carrying the debt beyond a specified period. So it's very easy to miss something in these deals that could derail your efforts.

We'll explain more about this in Chapter 9, "Save by Choosing the Right Loans."

Another option is to consolidate your debts by taking out a home equity loan or home equity line of credit, which we also discuss in more detail in Chapter 9. Interest on home equity loans or lines may be deductible on your income taxes, but using them to consolidate debt could present these problems:

- If you can't make your payments, the lender can take your house!
- If you're already debt-ridden and you're not careful, having yet another loan to tap could add to your debt.
- These loans, too, may come with hidden fees and/or higher rates, under certain conditions. Watch for upfront, annual, and/or termination fees.
- Expect to pay a higher interest rate if you've already had problems paying bills.

All this, if you're not careful, could delay efforts to reach your financial goals.

Bankruptcy

If your debt problems are serious and you have little or no income, it could be in your best interest to check whether you're a candidate for personal bankruptcy. By qualifying for Chapter 7 bankruptcy, which involves the sale of most of your assets, you might be able to wipe out all or most of your debts, and get a fresh start. To qualify, you have to meet a "means test" to prove your income is within certain state limits. Plus, it's possible you still might have to pay child support, alimony, fines, taxes, and/or certain student loans. But once you're clear of most debt, you can proceed to reach the goals you set for yourself and your family in Chapter 2, "Identifying Your Financial Goals."

Visit the website of the U.S. Department of Justice U.S. Trustee Program at www.usdoj.gov/ust and, under Bankruptcy Reform, click on Means Testing Information to see if there's

CAUTION Home equity loan programs that offer to lend you more than 100% of the value of your home often aren't worth it. You can't deduct loan interest on your income taxes for more than 100% of a home's value.

NOTE If bankruptcy prospects are attractive, you'll likely need a bankruptcy attorney. Search the backgrounds of bankruptcy attorneys at www.martindale.com and find one in your area. Can't go online? Get the *Martindale-Hubbell Law Directory* at your local public library. Can't afford a bankruptcy attorney? Contact some attorneys in your area and ask if they know of any lawyers who might offer "pro bono" or volunteer services. Other prospects to contact for potentially low-cost or free legal help are local legal aid societies and area university legal departments.

a chance you might qualify for Chapter 7 bankruptcy.

If you can't qualify for Chapter 7 bankruptcy, you might find some relief from creditors, foreclosures, repossessions, garnishments, and utility shutdowns under Chapter 13 of the bankruptcy code. With Chapter 13, the court approves a repayment plan, but you still have to pay off your debts within three to five years.

Again, remember to see a government-approved credit counseling agency within six months before filing bankruptcy.

> **CAUTION** Unless you follow all the rules and meet required income quotas, you could be ordered to pay back a good chunk of your debt. Furthermore, a bankruptcy remains on your credit record for 10 years, with certain exceptions. It can be reported longer in connection with credit transactions of at least $150,000, insurance transactions of at least $150,000, or employment involving an annual salary of at least $75,000.

Understanding Your Credit Score

We've told you how to get out of debt. But even if you have no debt, your credit score is an important number in your financial life. The reason: Lenders are no longer the only ones who look at it. Many insurance companies now examine credit scores. They may use this number, along with other factors, to determine your rates or even whether to insure you.

> **TIP** Debtors Anonymous is a self-help group set up like Alcoholics Anonymous. People with financial problems meet weekly in a group setting. The goal: to help people cope with and solve their debt problems. For more information, visit www.debtorsanonymous.org.

Believe it or not, your credit score could even affect your effort to get a job, rent an apartment, or sign up for a cell phone. Plus, more municipalities are turning over unpaid parking tickets, library fees, and other municipal bills that go unpaid to collection agencies. This can cause credit scores to drop.

By knowing your credit score and raising it as much as possible, you have a tool to obtain better credit terms, including lower interest rates, and perhaps better prices on insurance. It's also possible that a good credit score might save you from needing to shell out a security deposit for your utilities.

A credit score measures a number of factors on your credit report, including

- Your ability to pay your bills on time
- The number and type of loans
- Late payments

- Collection actions
- Total debts
- How long you have owed money

Credit scores generally range from about 300 to as high as 999, depending upon the company that issues the score and the specific type of score. A new type of credit score, known as the VantageScore, issues a credit score comprised of lettered grades.

TO DO LIST

- ❏ Find out your credit score
- ❏ Check your credit report
- ❏ Correct inaccuracies on your report
- ❏ Minimize credit blemishes

Getting Your Score

Nationwide consumer reporting agencies or credit bureaus are required to issue you, upon request, a copy of your credit score. The major consumer reporting agencies are

- Equifax: 800-685-1111; www.equifax.com
- Experian: 888-397-3742; www.experian.com
- TransUnion: 800-888-4213; www.transunion.com

The problems: There's more than one type of credit score, and you might not know which credit score your lender is using. Different credit scoring systems have different ranges and meanings. Some lenders and insurers may use their own internally devised credit score. If you want your credit score, you'll likely have to pay a fee, which can vary, depending upon your state laws and what else the credit bureaus insert in the package that includes your credit score.

Perhaps you've already heard of a credit score referred to as a *FICO score*. That stands for Fair Isaac Corp. (www.fairisaac.com) of Minneapolis, Minnesota—the most well-known nationwide provider of credit scores. Fair Isaac's most popular credit score ranges from 300 to 850. Fair Isaac's median credit score on that model is 723. In general, a bad credit score runs below 620. You also can purchase a credit score from Fair Isaac at www.myfico.com. Its cheapest price was $15.95, which includes not only your score but also a credit report. A number of other vendors may also offer credit scores, but they might not be the same scores used by lenders.

> **TIP** An analysis by Fair Isaac showed that if you applied for a $216,000 30-year fixed-rate mortgage, a great credit score of 760 to 850 could get you a low, 5.8% interest rate. By contrast, if your score ranged from 620 to 639, your interest rate would be 7.39%. The good credit score could save you $226 monthly on that mortgage! All that extra cash sure could go a long way toward reaching your financial goals.

Always keep in mind that your credit score likely is subject to change daily and may not be the sole reason for approval or denial of the financial service you seek.

You have some added protection if the lender uses a credit score to issue a mortgage or to refinance a home. In that case, the lender usually is required to disclose a credit score. Exceptions: if the loan is used for business, or if the lender buys a credit report that happens to have a credit score but doesn't use it. Although the lender is permitted to charge you for that score, the Real Estate Settlement Procedures Act—the federal law governing real estate settlement charges—prohibits the fee from being more than the lender paid for it. Lenders typically get credit scores in a package along with your credit reports.

> **CAUTION** If you're looking to qualify for a loan, make certain that the lender you select actually seeks business from people whose credit history is similar to yours. Ditto if you're seeking insurance. Some lenders, known as "subprime lenders," actually want to do business with people who have poor credit ratings. The reason: They can charge higher rates and make more profits on these loans. Other lenders may not want to have anything to do with any borrowers except those with the absolute best credit.

> **TIP** Even if the lender isn't required to disclose a credit score used in a loan you're seeking, it never hurts to ask what it is. Some lenders don't mind telling you.

Once you have an idea of your credit score and what it means, you can compare your interest rate with going interest rates, based on similar credit scores. One place to do it is www.myfico.com. Determine whether you're getting a fair deal. If not, tell your lender and ask for a lower rate, or shop around.

> **CAUTION** Not all credit scores come from Fair Isaac, so be certain to note who issued your score, and understand its true meaning, based on whatever system is used.

LENDERS CONSIDER OTHER THINGS

Your credit score often is not the only factor considered by a lender in its decision of whether to grant you a loan or other financial service. So don't give up the ship if your credit score is down in the dumps. If you've had a family medical emergency that derailed your credit, your lenders might consider this fact. Notify them in writing of your plight. In fact, as we wrote this book, some credit bureaus were adding notations on credit reports of borrowers who were victims of Hurricane Katrina. It was not yet known how this information ultimately would affect the borrowers' chances of qualifying for a loan.

What if you don't have a credit score?

Increasingly, lenders will consider you if you can document other regular business relationships and the fact that you've honored your obligations. Some, for example, might consider documentation of rent or utility payments, a checking account, or regular payments to a book club or record club. So shop around if you need a loan. We'll offer more tips on getting new credit and rebuilding credit in Chapter 9.

> **CAUTION** If you've only had credit for a short time, don't open lots of new credit card accounts. This can lower your credit score.

Check Your Credit Report to Raise Your Credit Score

Now that you understand credit scores and know certain factors that can lower yours, it's important to make every effort to raise it. Be sure to act way before you apply for any loan or financial service so that you're sure to get the best possible terms. The rules are simple:

- Get your credit reports from the three major credit bureaus and correct any errors.
- Get outdated information on your credit report removed.

Again, the following are the three major credit bureaus or consumer reporting agencies that issue credit reports:

- Equifax: 800-685-1111; www.equifax.com
- Experian: 888-397-3742; www.experian.com
- TransUnion: 800-888-4213; www.transunion.com

> **CAUTION** Never respond to emails offering free credit reports. Also, double-check that you've typed in the correct official website address—www.annualcreditreport.com—if you do get your free report online. The website already has been mimicked by "phishers" or imposters seeking your personal information.

GET YOUR CREDIT REPORT FREE!

There are several circumstances in which you may be entitled to free credit reports. Otherwise, you may have to write to the three consumer reporting agencies and pay as much as $9.50 for each copy of your credit file.

First, everyone is entitled to one free copy of a credit report annually from each of the three major credit bureaus. But don't call the credit bureaus for it or it likely won't be free. To qualify for a free report, you must visit www.annualcreditreport.com, call 877-322-8228, or send your request to Annual Credit Report Request Service, P.O. Box 105281, Atlanta, GA, 30348-5281.

Other circumstances under which you're entitled to a free credit report include the following:

- You've been denied a loan. Just ask your lender for the name and phone number of the consumer reporting agency that provided your credit report.
- You've been a victim of identity theft.
- You successfully dispute an item in your credit report that results in a change.
- You're on public assistance.

Get more details on your credit rights, including your rights to free credit reports, at www.ftc.gov. This website also has the most comprehensive information on dealing with identity theft.

Correcting Mistakes on Your Credit Report

Review your credit report for mistakes. If you find any, you'll need to write to the consumer reporting agency or credit bureau immediately. Include your full name and address, and clearly identify each wrong item.

Second, forward copies of any information, receipts, or data you have to confirm the error. Feel free to include a copy of the report with the questioned items circled. Send your letter by certified mail, return receipt requested, so that you can document what was received. Keep copies of everything you sent.

Here is a sample dispute letter offered by the Federal Trade Commission on its website (www.ftc.gov):

Date
Your Name
Your Address, City, State, Zip Code

Complaint Department
Name of Company
Address
City, State, Zip Code

Dear Sir or Madam:

I am writing to dispute the following information in my file. I have circled the items I dispute on the attached copy of the report I received.

This item (identify item(s) disputed by name of source, such as creditors or tax court, and identify type of item, such as credit account, judgment, etc.) is (inaccurate or incomplete) because (describe what is inaccurate or incomplete and why). I am requesting that the item be deleted (or request another specific change) to correct the information.

Enclosed are copies of (use this sentence if applicable and describe any enclosed documentation, such as payment records, court documents) supporting my position. Please investigate this (these) matter(s) and (delete or correct) the disputed item(s) as soon as possible.

Sincerely,
Your name

Enclosures: (List what you are enclosing.)

The consumer reporting agency is required to investigate the questionable items—usually within 30 days, unless it considers the dispute "frivolous."

If the information provider finds that the disputed information is wrong, it must notify all three major nationwide consumer reporting companies so that the information is corrected.

If you ask, the consumer reporting company or credit bureau must notify anyone who received your report in the recent past.

> **NOTE** If a consumer reporting agency fails to follow very specific rules and correct information on your report, call the office of your state attorney general. You can find a list of state attorneys general at www.naag.org.

HOW TO DEAL WITH CREDIT FILE ERRORS

What if you simply can't get a mistake on your credit report corrected? You can

- Write up to 100 words stating reasons for disputing the accuracy or completeness of a credit report item. Submit it to the consumer reporting agency. It must be added to your credit report at no charge.
- Resubmit the dispute to the consumer reporting agency, but only if you have additional documentation.
- Sue under the Fair Credit Reporting Act for negligent or willful noncompliance. If successful, you can get damages, court costs, and attorney fees.
- When applying for a loan, request in writing that a lender consider information indicating that the credit history being considered is inaccurate. The lender is required to consider it.

What If Your Bad Credit Score Is Accurate?

If you have a bad credit score, and it's accurate, you need to know exactly when the items that are triggering it legally must be removed. Then, it's up to you to make certain the consumer reporting agency removes them.

Accurate negative information may stay on your credit report for seven years. Bankruptcy information, as we told you earlier, may be reported for 10 years or, in certain cases, longer.

Information about an unpaid judgment against you typically can be reported for at least seven years. The following have no time limit:

- Information on criminal convictions.
- Information reported in response to an application for a job that pays more than $75,000 annually.
- Information reported because you've applied for more than $150,000 worth of credit or life insurance.

> **CAUTION** If your credit record is blemished, don't fall for scams that promise to fix your credit for an upfront fee. They're probably illegal. Also, beware of debt settlement companies that charge outrageous fees to negotiate with your lender. Often, you're better off just paying your debt or dealing with your lender yourself.

The good news is that many lenders still will grant you credit even with bad information on your credit report. So it pays to take steps to boost your credit score as much as possible.

Here are some more ways to do that, according to Fair Isaac Corp.:

- Pay bills on time.
- If you've missed payments, get current and stay current.
- Keep balances on credit cards and other revolving accounts low.
- Pay off debt rather than moving it around.
- Confine your shopping for a given loan within a focused period of time.

Once you've succeeded in getting your debt under control and removing negative information from your credit report, be sure to ask your creditors to lower their interest rates and/or fees. You'll definitely have more leverage to shop for better deals. Plus, you'll have a lot more money to earmark toward your financial goals!

Summary

In this chapter, we outlined your options for dealing with debt: handle it yourself, see a credit counseling agency, consolidate debts, or file bankruptcy. Also, we explained that today, more lenders, insurers, landlords, and utility companies are considering your "credit score," a three-digit number designed to predict your chances of paying your loan or bills. Your credit score not only can be a factor in whether to grant you a number of financial services, but also can influence the price you pay. Generally, the higher your credit score, the lower your loan rate and the more leverage you may have on insurance prices. To raise a genuinely bad credit score, you need to correct any mistakes on your credit reports and make sure accurate bad information is removed when it legally is required to expire. Improving your credit score can help you free up even more money to put toward your financial life. Now, on to building wealth!

II

Creating a Simple Investment Plan

4   Weighing the Pros and Cons of Simple Investment Options 51

5   Creating a Plan That Works for You 61

6   Protecting the Downside: Insurance and Other Safeguards 77

4

Weighing the Pros and Cons of Simple Investment Options

IN THIS CHAPTER:

◆ Understand how basic investments work

◆ Identify your investment personality

◆ Select the right types of investments

You've set financial goals. You've also started eliminating debt from your financial life. This chapter marks the start of a big turnaround. We'll show you how to proceed full-speed ahead toward reaching your financial goals. There's a trump card that can go a long way toward getting you there. It's called investing. But to use this tool correctly, you need to fully understand how it works.

To many people, *investing* is a scary word. We can recall our late grandfather shying away from any investment in which the value could fluctuate. To him, it all represented "Wall Street," the same place where investors jumped from skyscrapers during the Great Depression in 1929. But if you play your cards right, investing can work to your advantage. We can't promise there won't be another Great Depression. However, we can give you a few basic rules to make sure a market downturn doesn't drive you and your family crazy. That's our aim in this chapter.

Once you understand the basics, investing usually can get you where you want to be faster than you'd think. Now, that's great news for anybody's financial life!

TO DO LIST

- ❏ Understand short-term cash investments
- ❏ Know the ins and outs of bond investments
- ❏ Learn about investing in the stock market
- ❏ Learn the basic rules of investment

Understanding Basic Investments

Once you've accumulated your six months' worth of emergency cash, you might be ready to start investing. Before you do, it helps to understand a few basic categories of investments. That's what we talk about in this section.

Cash

This term does not always represent the cash you have in your wallet. It also can refer to short-term investments that mature in three months or less. These types of investments are considered among the lowest risk because there's very little time to lose any money. Cash investments may include things like U.S. Treasury bills, money market mutual funds, and bank certificates of deposit.

> **TIP** Have you just finished paying off a credit card, car loan, or mortgage? Why not continue making the exact same monthly payment, but this time to your savings account rather than to your lender? Even better, have it done automatically!

Perhaps the lowest-risk cash investments are Treasury bills, because they are directly backed by the U.S. government. Next in the low-risk category are bank deposits. Bank deposits are insured to $100,000 per person per bank by the U.S. government–backed Federal Deposit Insurance Corp. (FDIC).

Although cash investments generally are among the lowest risk, they have two major drawbacks:

- Over time, they have earned the least among basic investments—an average of 3% to 4% annually. At that rate, reaching your financial goals sure could be slow-going!
- These investments may not keep up with the rate of inflation, or escalating prices. Inflation has averaged about 3% annually.

Bonds

These are similar to loans. In essence, you loan a certain amount of money to either a company, the U.S. government, or a municipality for a specific term at a specific interest rate. At maturity, you get back your principal, plus you also receive interest payments, generally semiannually. Because bonds are longer-term investments, they have more time to decline in value than cash investments and they also carry higher risks. On the other hand, historically, bonds have returned a little more than cash investments—an average of 5.5% annually since 1926, according to Ibbotson Associates, Chicago. Bonds generally are lower risk than stocks, the next investment we'll be discussing. The reason: If the entity issuing a bond goes belly-up, bondholders get priority over stockholders when it comes to getting paid back from the issuer's remaining assets.

> **NOTE** Own bonds? Be prepared to see your total returns fluctuate generally between -4% and 14% annually, based on Ibbotson Associates data since 1926.

Besides the fact that the issuer of a bond could go belly-up, there are some added risks with bonds:

- If you must sell a bond prior to maturity, you could lose money. Bond yields move in the opposite direction of interest rates, so if rates rise, the actual value of the bond could drop. Of course, the opposite also could happen. Why is the behavior of bonds so flaky? Say you could buy a bond today that yields 10%. You certainly wouldn't want the 6% bond that Joe Smith was trying to unload through his broker, would you? The only thing poor Joe possibly could do to get anyone to buy his 6% bond is to lower the bond's price. On the other hand, if bonds today were yielding 4%, everyone would be clamoring for Joe's 6% bond. Joe likely could charge more for the bond than he paid for it!

- Issuers reserve the right to "call" bonds. This means you get your money back prior to maturity. If your bond is called, you'll get your principal back, but you'll have to reinvest your money at lower rates—something you might not want to do.

> **CAUTION** The higher the yield or return of an investment, the greater the risk. Is a bond investment promising 10% interest income when bank rates are no more than 4%? You can be sure that bond is issued by a company that could be on the verge of bankruptcy. That's a big risk!

While many bonds lack the backing of the U.S. government, you can buy U.S. Treasury bonds, which are backed by Uncle Sam. But even with U.S. Treasury bonds, you can lose principal if interest rates have risen and you sell them prior to maturity.

Stocks

With a stock, you're part owner of a corporation. Stocks are among the riskiest investment categories because you're sharing in the company's profits and losses. Plus, you get no government guarantee. On the other hand, stocks have performed about the best of the three investment categories over time. Since 1926, stocks have grown at an annual rate of nearly 11%, according to Ibbotson Associates. That's substantially more than bonds and cash investments. The bad news: At any given moment, you could lose your shirt from a stock investment.

> **NOTE** If you own stocks, be prepared to see your investments fluctuate generally in any given year from –12% to 32%, at least based on Ibbotson Associates' data since 1926.

Basic Investment Rules

If you have a retirement plan or a company 401(k), you may already own some of the basic investments we just discussed. Keep in mind there is great variety within each of those categories. Plus, there are other categories of investments that invest in stocks, bonds, and cash. Those include mutual funds and exchange-traded funds, which both pool investors' money. We'll explain more about them later in this chapter, and in Chapter 5, "Creating a Plan that Works for You."

Then again, there are totally different, more-complex categories of investments altogether! Regardless of which category you invest in, you could pick a dud or a star. So how can you possibly begin to select an investment?

Following are the most important points to understand when considering these individual investment categories:

- There is no utopian investment. Anyone can lose money in virtually anything. By the same token, any single investment also may perform extraordinarily at any given point in time.
- You're least likely to lose any money with cash investments, particularly CDs or Treasury bills. But they still carry a major risk: Cash investments, over time, may not pay you enough to keep up with inflation. This means that down the road, your money might not grow enough to cover your basic living costs.
- Stocks are riskier than bonds. Bonds are riskier than cash.

- Of any of these three categories—stocks, bonds, and cash—stocks have earned the most over a period of 10 years or more. In the short run, they also have lost the most. So if you're barely able to pay your bills, and can't afford to lose, stay far away from stocks!
- If you have at least 10 years to invest and a healthy savings balance to cover your emergencies, owning stocks usually can go a long way toward meeting your financial goals.
- Bonds don't always move in the same direction as stocks, so owning some bonds could help you earn a bit more than cash investments and also help cushion you against stock market losses.

Savvy Spending The last point brings us to perhaps the most important rule when it comes to investing: It's critical to "diversify," or own several different types of investments. This way, if one investment zigs, the other zags, so you cushion some of your losses. You generally don't want to own all stocks, all bonds, or all cash investments. There's a lot less risk if you own more than one category of investments, and more than one investment in each category!

How much you should own of each category depends on your investment personality.

PLAY IT SAFE

Investing is very different from casino gambling. We prefer much better odds, thank you. That's why, if you're just getting out of debt and have no savings, it's best to start investing by immediately paying yourself before you pay any bills. Put excess money you've been able to free up through our exercises in Chapter 1, "Examining Your Financial Condition," into a safe investment, such as a bank money market account or CD. Every month, have money withdrawn from your checking account and put into your bank account. Once you've accumulated enough cash to cover any emergency, you're ready to move on to other investments.

Down with Debt Avoid borrowing money to invest. This is a recipe for disaster for all but the most sophisticated investors. And, perhaps the biggest mistake people make is to invest on a hot tip or a suggestion from a friend or relative. Bad move. It's better to understand the historic range of performance that's typical of the type of investment you're considering. Only then can you zero in on the right investments for you.

What Kind of Investor Are You?

Now that you understand both the risks and potential returns you can expect from stocks, bonds, and cash investments, it's important to establish how much of your money to keep in each category. After that, we'll help you nail down your choices even further.

Here's an easy benchmark. Subtract your age from 100. The result gives you a rough idea of about how much you should have in stocks. Keep the rest in bonds and/or cash. For example, if you're 30 years old, you might consider keeping 70% in stocks and 30% in bonds and cash. If you're 80 years old, consider keeping just 20% in stocks and 80% in bonds and/or cash.

Keep in mind that this is only a benchmark. Some believe this formula is too conservative. That could be. That's why it's so important to adjust this benchmark upward or downward, depending upon how much risk you think you can stomach.

The following questions may help you tweak this benchmark even further:

- How old are you?

    The younger you are, the more money you likely can afford to invest in stocks. Historically, the stock market has grown at more than 10% annually over the past seven decades. But stocks lose money one out of every three years, so you need a few years to make back your losses. The older you are, the more you need to keep what you have, so invest more in less risky investments, like bank CDs and bonds.

- How much are you willing to see the value of your investment decline in any given year?

    Would it really upset you to see your investments drop 10% over, say, a year, in exchange for potentially greater returns later on? If not, consider yourself aggressive. Might you tolerate no more than a 5% loss in your investments? If so, consider yourself conservative. Can't handle any loss at all? You're definitely safety minded. If you're safety-minded, about your only investment options are federally insured bank CDs and U.S. Treasury bills or bonds, backed by Uncle Sam. On the other hand, aggressive investors might keep more in stocks.

- How much time do you have before you'll need your investment?

> **CAUTION** Avoid investing in a single stock. Bad news about a company can send its stock tumbling. If you own several stocks, bad news about one company likely won't hurt your overall holdings.

CHAPTER 4 Weighing the Pros and Cons of Simple Investment Options

Are you saving to buy a vacation home in a few years or to live the good life in 30 years? You don't want to take any risk with your money on any investment for a short-term goal in a few years. Stay away from stocks! But if you have more than 5 or 10 years to invest, you might consider putting some money in a lower-risk stock investment or in a combination of bonds and stocks. Review the financial goals you set up based upon Chapter 2, "Identifying Your Financial Goals," so that you choose the right investments for your deadlines.

- Are you depending on income from your investments to live on?

  If so, stick mainly with bank CDs, short-term U.S. Treasury bills, Treasury bonds, and other income-producing investments. Don't need your investments for income? In that case, reinvest any income you get from your investments for the long term.

- How important is it to make sure the value of your investments keeps pace with the rising prices?

  Investments that typically keep pace with inflation include stocks, precious metals, and real estate. The older you are, however, the less you may want to keep in stocks and other volatile investments.

Here are some suggested investment mixes, based on certain situations. We'll also show you what you might expect from each investment mix in the way of performance, based on history.

- If you have at least 10 years to invest and can afford to take a loss now and then in exchange for superior returns long-term, you might consider investing about 80% in stocks and 20% in bonds. This type of split generally is recommended for people who are younger than 55 years old. Historically, since 1926, this investment mix has grown at over 9.8% annually. It registered one bad year for every four good ones. The average loss of this mix in a down year was –10%. But the worst one-year loss, in 1931, was –36%.

- Typically, people who have more than 5 to 10 years to invest and are at least 40 years old should consider a mix of 40% in bonds and 60% in stocks. Historically, this mix has grown at just under 9% annually since 1926. In

> **CAUTION** As we wrote this book, many economists were predicting that the stock market might not do quite as well over the next several years as it has done in the past. So you might want to be a bit more conservative. That means keeping a bit less in stocks.

addition, this investment mix has had one bad year for every four good ones. The average loss in a down year was –8%. The worst one-year loss, in 1931, was –28%.

- Investors who are conservative, typically at least 60 years old and with at least five years to invest, might keep 20% in cash, 40% in bonds, and 40% in stocks. Historically, this mix has grown at a 7.6% annual rate since 1926. This investment mix typically has one bad year for every five good ones. The average loss in a down year was –5%. The worst one-year loss, in 1931, was –19%.

- Income investors, anyone who is retired and needs income to live on in addition to Social Security and pension, might consider 20% in cash, 20% in stocks, and 60% in bonds. Historically, since 1926, this investment mix has grown at a 6.3% annual rate and typically has one bad year for every six good ones. The average loss in a down year was just –3%. The worst one-year loss, in 1931, was –12%.

Once you've gotten a feel for your money personality and how various mixes of investments have performed over time, consider determining your own investment mix. Insert your own suitable investment mix, based on the benchmarks and suggestions we described earlier, as well as your own temperament for risk, here:

Stocks_____Bonds_____Cash_____

When you can split up your investments so that you get the best return with the least amount of risk for your situation, it's easier to start thinking about setting up your own investment plan.

SELECTING YOUR INVESTMENTS

Still not feeling quite like legendary investors such as Warren Buffett and Peter Lynch? Don't despair. Once you've determined the investment mix that's right for you, it's much easier to hire your very own money manager. You can do this independently. Refer to Appendix B, "Finding the Right Help," to assist you in selecting a money manager or financial planner. You also can hire a money manager simply by investing in mutual funds or exchange-traded funds.

Even if you hire someone else to manage your investments, always know exactly which types of investments are in any fund you're considering and, as we just discussed, whether they fit your age and investment personality. You can't always rely on a fund's name. Nor can you always rely completely on your money manager.

Investing in Mutual Funds and Exchange-Traded Funds

Both mutual funds and exchange-traded funds are an easy way to do your own investing in baskets of stocks, bonds, cash, and other investments. You pay an annual fee, expressed as a percentage of assets. The great thing about these types of investments is that if bad news about one of the fund's holdings sends it plummeting, you have other investments in the funds to cushion the blow. You might better recognize exchange-traded funds through their odd-sounding names, such as iShares, QQQs, SPDRs, (pronounced "Spiders") and Vipers.

Here are the chief differences between mutual funds and exchange-traded funds:

- Exchange-traded funds must be purchased through a stock broker, so you pay a commission. Mutual funds can be purchased a variety of ways: through a broker, for a "load" or commission; through a discount broker's "fund supermarket," with no commission but perhaps higher annual expenses; or directly from the mutual fund's investment company with no load or commission.

- Exchange-traded funds may be traded continuously on a stock exchange. Mutual fund transactions are settled just once—at the end of the day.

- Exchange-traded funds typically generate less taxable income than mutual funds because most are invested in the stocks or bonds that make up published indexes, such as the S&P 500. On the other hand, mutual funds may buy and sell investments, generating capital gains taxes on the trades. However, certain mutual funds do aim to keep their taxes low. Those may be competitive with exchange-traded funds, tax-wise.

> **NOTE** Even if you pay no load or commission to a broker for your fund, more so-called "no-load" mutual funds may charge "redemption fees" if you cash out within a certain time frame. Plus, you could pay fees if your balance drops below a certain threshold. Before you invest, be sure to read a fund's "prospectus" or legal offering document, which discusses fees, strategy, and risks.

- Unlike mutual funds, new exchange-traded funds are not limited to stock and bond investments. Some let you invest, for example, in gold directly through a custodial relationship with a bank. On the other hand, it may be tough to find an exchange-traded fund that invests in certain bonds, for example. Also, exchange-traded funds, which debuted in 1989, have not been around as long as mutual funds.

Which of these two types of pooled investments you might choose depends upon several factors, including the nature of investment you're seeking, how often you're trading, and your tax situation.

All the investments discussed in this chapter—stocks, bonds, cash, mutual funds, and exchange traded funds—are known as *securities*. In fact, so is virtually any investment contract in which you expect to profit through the efforts of someone else. The good news is that federal laws require companies publicly offering securities for investment to tell the truth about their businesses, the securities they are selling, and investment risks. Also, they require those who trade securities to treat investors fairly and honestly, putting investors first.

Summary

This chapter offers a few rules of thumb when it comes to investing. Always start with an emergency fund to cover your immediate expenses. Keep it safe—like a bank money market account, for example. Stocks are riskier than bonds, which are I.O.U.s. Bonds are riskier than cash investments, which mature in three months or less. If you need all your money to pay monthly bills, stay far away from stocks. If you have more room to maneuver, stocks historically have paid more than other investments over a term of at least 10 years. Beware that the value of your bond can drop if you need to sell it after interest rates have risen.

Cash investments and bonds can help cushion stock market losses. By diversifying, or owning a mix of different kinds of investments, you can cushion your losses while increasing earnings. How much you should put in stocks, bonds, or cash depends on your age, financial goals, and the amount of risk you can handle.

Mutual funds and exchange-traded funds offer easy ways to help you diversify automatically into stocks, bonds, and cash. With both, you can own a pool of stocks or bonds. You pay an annual management fee.

In the next chapter, we'll zero in more specifically on picking the right investments and give you some easy investment strategies.

5

Creating a Plan That Works for You

IN THIS CHAPTER:
- Getting the highest yields with the lowest risk
- Using the easiest ways to diversify
- Keeping fees low and earnings high

You've just determined about how much you can tolerate investing in stocks, bonds, and cash investments. Now, it's time to bring out the list of goals you created for your financial life in Chapter 2, "Identifying Your Financial Goals." Remember? You figured out how much you and your family will need and when you'll need it. For now, put what may be your largest expenses —your children's education and your own retirement—on the back burner. We have special tips for those goals later in the book.

In this chapter, we hit your chief objective: meeting your financial goals. To do this, you need to earn the most you possibly can. On the other hand, you need to avoid a major drop in the value of your investments just when you need money. That's why we'll help you determine more specifically which investments to consider, based on your goals. We'll also show you how to find the best deals on them and offer strategies to grow your wealth fast, minimize your losses, and cut your taxes.

TO DO LIST

- ❏ Learn about the best low-risk investments
- ❏ Track down the best bank deposit earnings
- ❏ Invest in U.S. Treasury securities
- ❏ Find other low-risk investment opportunities

Choose Low-Risk Investments for Short-Term Goals

Stick first with the goals you'd like to meet relatively soon—say, in less than three years. For those, you need to stay largely with some of the lowest-risk investments, like cash and, perhaps, bonds. That's because you can't afford any market downturns on money you need so soon. Here's what to consider.

Bank Deposits

Savvy Spending

Good old-fashioned bank deposits may be one of your safest bets, and it's possible to find banks that will let you invest as little as $25 or so if you shop around. With bank deposits, your principal and interest are guaranteed by the U.S. government–backed Federal Deposit Insurance Corporation (FDIC) to $100,000 per person per bank. By doing a little shopping, you usually can give yourself a major raise. For example, the same-day money market accounts/savings accounts earned a national average yield of 3.20%, according to Bankrate.com; we found yields as high as 4.55%. That's the objective. You want to earn as much as humanly possible with the least amount of risk for your financial life! Have five years to invest? You can boost your yield even further by taking out a five-year CD. We recently found one outfit at Bankrate.com paying 5.05%. That's nearly 2 percentage points more than the average money market account yield!

> **CAUTION** Although CDs normally pay higher rates than money market accounts or savings accounts, they have penalties for early withdrawal. Also, expect to pay fees on savings or money market accounts if you fall below a minimum balance or exceed allotted transactions.

Online, you can find yields that are available nationally. But sometimes, banks offer special deals locally that may not be available online. So it also pays to call around to your local banks and check ads in your area newspapers. Also shop credit unions. Credit unions typically pay a little more on their CDs. You can visit the Credit Union National Association at www.cuna.org and click on "Visit Our Credit Union Locator" or call 800-358-5710 to track down a credit union you might be eligible to join. Federally insured credit unions, provided that they are insured through the National Credit Union Administration (NCUA), have the same U.S. government protection in the event of a failure as banks.

> **TIP** It's possible to lock into a one-year CD only to find interest rates rising. One way around this problem is to "ladder" your terms. In other words, divide your money into CDs of different terms so that you have money maturing periodically.

TIPS ON OPENING OUT-OF-TOWN BANK ACCOUNTS

Often banks located in other cities and states pay higher rates than local banks.

If you're comfortable dealing with an out-of-state institution, call the bank toll-free. Make sure you write down the name of the bank representative that helps you. If possible, reserve an account number, and ask that the account information be mailed or emailed to you. Complete the forms, and send them along with a check via mail with return receipt requested. You also can wire money from your bank or brokerage firm to the bank, but expect to be charged—possibly by both the sender and receiver—for this service. Make copies of all documents. Keep the confirmation of your investment in a safe place. Make sure your loved ones know about the account.

Be smart about choosing an out-of-town bank, however. Make certain it is legitimate by first checking that it exists at www.fdic.gov. Keep in mind that it could be tougher to access your money or get a customer service representative in the event of a disaster or theft. Also, while the FDIC covers you if the bank fails, it generally does not cover theft. Although many banks do reimburse defrauded customers, some customers have to take their banks to court to get their money back.

You also can buy a CD outside your area through a broker, but most broker-sold CDs don't permit early withdrawals. If you must sell your CD through your broker prior to maturity, you could take a major loss because the value of the CD fluctuates. Also be sure you don't already have cash at the same institution that could put you over the $100,000 FDIC insurance limit. Keep good records of your account in case the institution fails, and only deal with reputable companies.

So it pays to research a bank or other financial institution you're considering at websites such as www.ripoffreport.com, www.consumeraffairs.com, and www.complaints.com. Also, check with the entity's regulator, and use an online search engine, such as Google, to learn as much as you can about the institution.

U.S. Treasury Securities

For the lowest-risk investments—even lower-risk than bank deposits—turn to the U.S. government. Treasury securities are backed directly by Uncle Sam. If all else fails and the economy nosedives, Uncle Sam can print more money to make absolutely sure you get your principal returned. Plus, interest on Treasury securities is exempt from state and local income taxes.

Most Treasury securities require a minimum investment of $1,000. Treasury bills, or T-bills, have maturities of 4 weeks, 13 weeks, and 26 weeks. These are sold at a discount to face value. This means you might pay, say, $970 for a $1,000 T-bill. The difference, which you receive at maturity, is your interest.

Treasury notes come in terms of 2, 3, 5, and 10 years. Treasury bonds are longer term—up to 30 years. Notes and bonds pay interest every six months.

Treasury Inflation-Protected Securities (TIPS), another Uncle Sam–backed security designed to protect you from inflation, had terms of 5, 10, and 20 years at this writing. The return fluctuates based on inflation, as measured by the Consumer Price Index. At maturity, you receive the adjusted principal or the original principal, whichever is greater.

U.S. SAVINGS BONDS HAVE LOWER MINIMUMS

You can invest as little as $25 in a Series EE U.S. savings bond, which, at this writing, has a fixed interest rate, or a Series I bond, which has a variable rate, based on inflation.

With both types of U.S. savings bonds, interest is added to the bond monthly and paid when you cash in the bond. Both may earn interest for 30 years, but you are charged a penalty—three months of interest—if you withdraw within the first five years.

With both types of bonds, you pay federal income taxes on your earnings when you cash them in. But if you meet income and other qualifications, you get to exclude any earnings that are used to finance education from your federal income tax.

Unlike I bonds, paper EE bonds are sold at one-half of the face value. After 20 years, the value of your EE bond automatically doubles. At that point, the U.S. Treasury can change the interest rate for the remaining 10 years.

Don't want to invest electronically? In that case, you'll need to pony up $50 to buy an I bond.

The terms of U.S. savings bond offerings sometimes change, so double-check them at www.treasurydirect.gov.

You can obtain Treasury securities from a Federal Reserve Bank, a bank, or online at www.treasurydirect.gov. Treasury securities—excluding U.S. savings bonds—also may be purchased through a broker. But the value may fluctuate based on interest rates as well as supply and demand. Also, expect a broker to take a cut, built into the bond's price, as payment.

Other Lower-risk Investments

Want to try to earn a little more? As we indicated in the prior chapter, bonds may be the way to go. But once you invest in bonds that aren't issued by the U.S. Treasury, you're getting away from a guarantee of the man—Uncle Sam. Corporations issue bonds to raise money. If the company goes belly-up, you could lose your investment.

You also may lose principal if you need to sell a U.S. government, corporate, or municipal bond. That's because bond prices and interest rates move in the opposite direction. When interest rates rise, bond prices fall. Because bonds have these added risks, they generally tend to pay higher yields.

There are different types of bonds. Some are riskier than others. We already told you that the lowest-risk bonds are those issued by the U.S. Treasury—provided that you hold them to maturity. That's because Uncle Sam guarantees them. Next up, municipal bonds. These are issued by cities, states, and other government entities. The great thing about municipal bonds is that they're not subject to federal income tax and some may even be state-tax free. So, if you're in a high tax bracket, municipal bonds are worth considering. However, they generally yield less than other types of bonds, so if you're not paying high taxes, look elsewhere.

CAUTION Always double-check tax consequences of Treasury securities. If you buy certain types of securities through a broker, you may be required to pay income taxes on interest even though you don't get it until maturity. Also, in certain cases, even though state and local income taxes aren't owed, inheritance, estate, or other types of state and local taxes may be due on the earnings.

CAUTION Bonds are tricky! The longer a bond's term, the higher the yield, but the more you can expect its value to drop if rates rise and you need to sell it. Say interest rates rise 1%. The value of a 30-year U.S. Treasury bond would decline 11.58%. By contrast, a five-year Treasury note would lose just 4.75%. On the other hand, if interest rates declined, the value of your bonds could grow just as much!

A select number of municipal bonds are backed by insurance companies, such as the Municipal Bond Investors Assurance Corporation (MBIA), American Municipal Bond Assurance Corporation (AMBAC), or Financial Guaranty Insurance Company (FGIC). The insurers pay both principal and interest on an insured municipal bond in the event of a default. MBIA, AMBAC, and FGIC only guarantee the financially strongest bonds, rated single A to AAA by Standard & Poor's and Moody's.

> **CAUTION** Always evaluate the financial strength of a bond you're considering, and don't be confused about the grading system. Although a B grade in school generally is above average, a B credit rating for a bond means it's high risk! Investment-grade bonds, on the other hand, are rated A to AAA by Standard & Poor's and Moody's Investors Service.

As we wrote this book, a number of municipalities were having financial problems, so be sure to check credit ratings and research available very carefully if you're considering a bond. Bonds rated AAA by Standard & Poor's and Aaa by Moody's represent the strongest issuers. The riskiest are those rated below BBB.

Online Advisor

If you want to find an online calculator to determine if the tax benefit of a municipal bond is worth the lower interest rate when compared with a taxable bond, visit www.investinginbonds.com.

Want a little higher yield? Corporate bonds typically yield the most of all types of bonds. But that's because corporate bonds, as we told you earlier, also are among the riskiest of your bond categories. "High yield" or "junk bonds" are the riskiest types of corporate bonds. They're issued by companies with poor credit ratings. Generally, they're rated below BBB, although standards may vary. Don't put money you can't afford to lose into junk bonds. Bondholders, though, get paid out of a company's remaining assets before stockholders.

Savvy Spending

Earlier, we told you about the concept of laddering CDs—you buy them at different terms so you have some money maturing at various intervals. This strategy works even better with individual bonds because bonds tend to be longer term. By laddering, you roll over the

> **TIP** After putting away a healthy amount of money in a savings account, why not consider laddering some CDs and/or bonds? You can have them mature at different terms equal to the number of years in which you might need the money to reach your financial goals. Example: Say you'll need a vacation in one year and a car in seven years. Split up your available cash into a one-year CD and a seven-year CD or bond. You'll be able to take advantage of generally higher longer-term rates and still have money when you need it!

money into new bonds that pay higher yields if rates are rising. Or, if rates drop, at least you'll still be earning the higher yields of your longer-term bonds on some of your money. Plus, laddering provides a way to avoid locking up all your money at once. You have money maturing periodically.

Stocks: More Risk for Better Long-Term Returns

If you're looking to improve your financial life, stocks can be a great help, although they're the riskiest of basic investment categories. Some types of stocks are riskier than others.

For example, you might have heard stocks categorized as *large-cap*, *mid-cap*, and *small-cap*. These categories refer to the company's "capitalization" or size, based on the market value of all outstanding shares of stock. Small-cap stocks typically are those of smaller or newer companies with less history in the marketplace. Small-cap stocks tend to be riskier than large-cap stocks, which more commonly are those of larger, better-established companies.

Growth stocks have fast-growing earnings. They are more volatile than *income* stocks, which are lower-risk stocks that pay periodic high dividends or profits to shareholders. *Value* stocks tend to sell at lower prices in relation to earnings, representing a potential bargain.

There's good reason to bother explaining all these different categories and characteristics. Earlier, we told you how important it is to diversify your investments—between stocks, bonds, and cash. Knowing the nature or category of a stock, bond, or cash investment helps you to diversify your holdings within each popular type of investment category as well.

However, rather than confuse your financial life with all these individual types of securities, why not hire professionals to do this for you? We'll show you how to do that next.

TO DO LIST

- ❏ Learn to invest in mutual funds
- ❏ Understand the risks of mutual funds
- ❏ Choose life-cycle and target funds

Choose Mutual Funds to Help You Diversify

Fortunately, there's no need today to stress out about which stocks or bonds to buy. A much simpler approach—mutual funds—is available. Mutual funds are pools of investor money, complete with professional management. With them, you can cash out when you want.

The objective of a mutual fund is to make more for shareholders. Because a mutual fund likely owns a large number of stocks and/or bonds, you're immediately cutting one significant risk of investing: the fact that bad news about a company could immediately sink the value of one stock or bond.

Analyzing the Risk of Mutual Funds

Before you invest in any mutual fund, it's important to determine what type of investments it contains, so you have an idea of how risky the fund is. The following are some types of mutual funds, listed very generally from some of the most risky to some of the least risky. However, beware that any one of these funds can lose or gain significantly more than this list may indicate based on market conditions or a host of other factors.

- Funds that invest in stocks of one type of industry, such as technology or gold-mining stocks
- Diversified stock funds
- Funds that invest in high-yield or "junk bonds"
- Funds that invest in corporate bonds

> **NOTE** Whenever you're considering a mutual fund, you need to read the prospectus so that you know its strategy and see exactly what types of investments are in the fund. Also, be sure to understand the risks and consider the tax consequences. Don't just go by its name. Ask for the statement of additional information, which may let you know if a fund engages in any high-risk strategies.

> **NOTE** Mutual fund companies promise to keep money market mutual fund share prices at $1, so, unlike with bond mutual funds, you shouldn't lose any money if rates rise. But remember: Any guarantee is only as good as the mutual fund company behind it.
>
> Don't confuse money market funds with bank money market accounts, which are FDIC-insured savings accounts. There have been more than 50 cases where money market mutual funds have lost money. Their fund families have had to kick in cash so investors did not lose principal. At least one money fund actually closed its doors, leaving its investors, primarily community banks, with a loss of 4 cents on the dollar.
>
> Don't confuse money market funds with short-term bond funds, either. With short-term bond funds your principal typically fluctuates slightly.

- Funds that invest in U.S. Treasury securities
- Money market mutual funds that invest in cash investments, with an average maturity of 90 days or less

Mutual funds also may invest internationally. Owning an international fund can help reduce risk when combined with U.S. investments. Reason: International stock and bond investments don't always move in the same direction as U.S. stocks and bonds.

Pinpoint Your Strategy with Life-Cycle and Target Funds

Want to take on some risk but feel uncomfortable picking your own investments? Major mutual fund families today have funds that do it for you automatically. Example: You make one investment in a fund aimed at your particular stage of life. The fund company picks your mutual funds, often a mix of stock and bond funds, and manages the process for you.

Or, set a date at which you need the money. The mutual fund company does the rest. These are known, respectively, as "life-cycle" and "target" funds.

But these mutual funds vary dramatically in terms of the mix of investments they contain, so read the prospectus carefully. Some are riskier than others. So you want to make certain their mix of stocks, bonds, and cash is in line with the mix you set for yourself in

CAUTION If safety is critical, always invest directly in a bond, CD, or U.S. Treasury security rather than a mutual fund that contains these investments! When you invest in a mutual fund that includes bonds or cash investments—even if it includes U.S. Treasury securities—you're taking on more risk. That's because you no longer have the same guarantee by the issuer that you'll get your principal back at maturity. When a bond matures, you get your principal back. But bond funds don't mature. A fund manager may be trading these investments, so your share price can fluctuate.

NOTE Morningstar, Inc. Chicago, is considered the most prominent mutual fund research service. Target funds recommended by Morningstar include the Vanguard Target Retirement Fund and the Fidelity Freedom Fund. Morningstar-recommended life-cycle funds include T. Rowe Price's Personal Strategy Funds and Vanguard Life Strategy. Morningstar's Mutual Fund Screener lets you compare mutual funds. The website helps you analyze a fund, based on investment category, risk, fees, and performance. You can obtain reports and valuable statistics. There also are educational articles to help you make decisions. See Appendix A, "References and Resources," for more helpful resources.

Chapter 4, "Weighing the Pros and Cons of Simple Investment Options."

Take a More Conservative Approach with Balanced Funds

Another easy solution if you're queasy about investing beyond the guarantee of Uncle Sam may be balanced funds. These mutual funds have a relatively equal split of stocks and bonds.

Historically, balanced funds have grown at about an 8% annual rate, but on the downside, they've lost half as much as the overall stock market. If the stock market drops about 10%, a balanced fund is apt to drop about 5% to 6%.

CAUTION Life-cycle and target funds all are relatively new. Some have more fees than others. Plus, when selecting one of these funds, it is important to recalculate your investment mix, adding in investments you already own.

TIP Vanguard Wellington, Dodge & Cox Balanced Fund, and Fidelity Balanced Fund are balanced funds with good long-term track records, according to Morningstar.

TO DO LIST
- ❑ Cut costs with no-load funds
- ❑ Reduce expenses with index funds
- ❑ Minimize costs of actively managed funds
- ❑ Try automatic investing with dollar cost averaging
- ❑ Periodically rebalance investments

Boost Your Performance

Here are some simple rules that can help you to increase mutual fund performance dramatically—no matter what type of funds you choose.

Stick with No-Load Funds

Savvy Spending You can immediately improve your investment performance by cutting fees. There are two major types of fees to watch:

CHAPTER 5   Creating a Plan That Works for You   71

- *Loads* or commissions, which you typically pay if you buy your fund from a broker or financial advisor.
- Annual expenses, expressed as an *expense ratio*, or percentage of a fund's assets.

How much you pay for your mutual funds is up to you. So why not go the cheapest route?

You can avoid mutual fund loads or commissions entirely simply by buying a no-load mutual fund directly from the mutual fund company or from certain discount brokerages. The drawback of buying mutual funds directly: If you're worried about picking the right funds, you may not get as much hand-holding as you would through a broker or financial advisor.

> **NOTE** Funds bought through a discount brokerage might have higher annual expenses than if they were purchased directly from the fund group.

Research indicates you'll get no worse management, and perhaps even better management, with no-load funds than with funds that charge "loads." That's on top of lower fees. This is a winning combination. Some of the most well-known no-load mutual fund families include the following:

- Vanguard, 800-523-0857, www.vanguard.com
- Fidelity Investments, 800-544-8888, www.fidelity.com
- T. Rowe Price, 800-541-8803, www.troweprice.com
- American Century Investments, 800-345-2021, www.americancentury.com

> **TIP** Consider no-load, low-cost index funds offered by the Vanguard Group, www.vanguard.com. You don't pay a commission to invest in these funds. Plus, Vanguard funds have the lowest annual expenses, according to Morningstar.
>
> If you prefer to go through a financial advisor, some of the best-performing commission-based funds are offered by American Funds (www.americanfunds.com), MFS Investment Management (www.mfs.com), and the Oppenheimer Funds (www.oppenheimerfunds.com).

Online Advisor: For a more detailed list of no-load mutual fund companies, visit the Mutual Fund Education Alliance at www.mfea.com and click on Direct No-Load under How to Buy Mutual Funds. That website also provides tools that let you track down funds with the lowest annual management fees.

Use Index Funds

Another way to cut fund expenses is to invest in low-cost *index* mutual funds. These types of mutual funds invest directly in the investments that are contained in published indexes that track a particular type of security. For example, many mutual fund families have an index fund that invests in the Standard & Poor's 500 index. That's a published index that tracks the stock market, based on the performance of 500 large stocks.

You needn't pay a commission to invest in index funds. And because the manager isn't employing any unusual skills, annual expenses often are among the lowest.

Over the past 20 years, the Vanguard 500 Index Fund has outperformed over 60% of all actively managed stock funds. So why bother racking your brains over which stock or stock fund will outperform the market from year to year? Just invest in the stock market itself.

A bond fund index that tracks the overall performance of the bond market is the Lehman Brothers U.S. Aggregate Bond Index.

Virtually all major mutual fund families have index funds—including no-load funds. Which you choose depends upon the amount of time you have to invest and the amount of risk you'd like to take. We told you about the S&P 500 index funds, which invest in large company stocks. But you also can find several other types of index funds. There are index funds that invest in stocks that make up the total stock market, and many types of bond indexes.

> **CAUTION** The downside of index funds is that their managers won't bail you out if your mutual fund's value suddenly plunges. That's why it's critical to diversify. Once you own a stock index fund, for example, make sure you also own a bond index fund. You also need to have a sufficient amount of money in cash to be sure to meet your everyday expenses in case your investments fluctuate. Not all index funds have low fees, either. So it still pays to compare expenses, which are summarized in the prospectus as "expense ratios."

Opting for Actively Managed Funds

Don't like our philosophy of sticking with index funds? If you prefer to invest in actively managed mutual funds, here are the factors to compare with similar funds, so you know you're getting the best performance:

- How has the fund performed over the past 1-, 3-, 5-, and 10-year periods based on its annual rate of return?
- How has the fund performed year by year in both up and down markets? Be sure to examine 2000, 2001, and 2002 when the stock market lost

almost 50%. How did the fund perform in up markets in 1995 through 1999?

- How much does the fund cost? Check the fund's annual expenses. Also, do you pay a "load" or commission?
- How has the fund performed versus the fund's category average? For example, you want to compare a large company growth stock fund with the growth stock fund averages. You can find these at www.morningstar.com.
- Does the fund own stocks, bonds, or both? Does it own any other types of investments? How has the fund performed versus the stock market or bond market averages? You probably can find much of this information at websites such as www.morningstar.com, www.marketwatch.com, and http://finance.yahoo.com.

Consider Dollar Cost Averaging

Now that you have an inkling of which types of funds may be best for your goals and, perhaps, have settled on a fund family, set your investment plan on automatic. Have whatever fund or funds you select automatically deduct a fixed amount monthly from your savings or checking account. Invest it in the mutual fund or mutual funds you've selected, based on your goals. You won't even realize the money is gone, and you'll reach your goals faster than you think!

Dollar cost averaging may not perform as well as a lump-sum investment if the market is rising. But it's great protection against a downturn! When the market tanks, you'll be buying shares at a lower price when the value is down. Over the long term, the average cost of your investment should prove lower than the current price.

> **TIP** Dollar cost averaging works great with mutual funds that invest in stocks.

Rebalance Your Investments

In Chapter 4, "Weighing the Pros and Cons of Simple Investment Options," we had you determine which proportion of your investments to keep in stocks, bonds, and cash. As markets gyrate, expect those proportions to get whacked out. Rebalancing means that periodically—say, at least once a year—you take profits from your best-performing investments and reinvest them in your poor-performing investments until your proportions are back on track. This technique forces you to take profits and reinvest them in underperforming investments while their prices are lower.

Example: Say you decided to keep 60% of your money in stocks or stock mutual funds and 40% in bonds or bond mutual funds. At the end of every year, make sure you have this same mix.

Always Consider Taxes

Unfortunately, when you make money in virtually any investment, Uncle Sam also wants a take. Your objective: When it comes to taxes, stay far away as possible from this man! Unfortunately, the U.S. Congress hasn't made this easy. Even the IRS's own employees can't figure out all the crazy tax rules. So how do they expect us to do it? Then, of course, you also must consider state and local taxes.

At this writing, you generally are charged a maximum 15% on capital gains—profits you get from the sale of investments you've held at least one year. Taxes on gains of assets you've held less than one year are taxed at your regular income tax rate. Dividends, or distributions of earnings to shareholders, also are taxed at a maximum 15% rate, with one major exception: Dividends on bond and money market mutual funds are considered interest, and are taxed at your regular income tax rate.

Bottom line: Check with your accountant. But here are a few pointers we've picked up along the way that can help minimize taxes on your investments:

- If your tax bracket is higher than 15%, consider keeping bonds, money market accounts, and real estate types of mutual funds in tax-sheltered accounts, such as retirement accounts, which we'll discuss more in Chapter 7, "Saving for Retirement."
- Have you lost money in a stock or mutual fund? You can offset capital losses against capital gains, so you pay less tax. This means, for example, that if you're looking to take profits on a stock or stock mutual fund, consider also selling another investment that's a dud.
- You can't deduct a loss if you buy the same stock back within 30 days after you sold it. This gets complicated, but it's known as the *wash sale rule*.
- Never buy a mutual fund at the end of the year without first checking what's known as its *ex-dividend* date. When you sell a mutual fund, you

must pay taxes not only on capital gains, but also, as a shareholder, on your mutual fund's profits. Those profits often are distributed to shareholders at year end. Avoid them altogether by buying the fund after profits are distributed!
- Are you in a high tax bracket? Consider tax-free municipal bonds or bond funds as well as tax-managed funds, available through most mutual fund groups.

Summary

In this chapter, you learned investment ideas to help you reach your long-term goals.

If you can't afford to lose any money, stay away from stocks, which are among the riskiest of investments. On the other hand, stocks have performed the best over the long term and can prove an attractive way to reach your goals over 10 years or more.

You may increase your return and lower your risk by diversifying—owning different types of investments, such as stocks and bonds. Mutual funds can provide an easy way to do this. These liquid, professionally managed pools of money own several investments. This way, if one investment does poorly, your entire investment won't necessarily tank.

Whenever you invest in a mutual fund, you need to know the nature of investments in the fund, and whether you can handle the risk. You can save money and increase performance by sticking with no-load mutual funds, which you can buy directly from a no-load mutual fund company. Index funds also are among the lowest-cost mutual funds, but remember that they offer no fund manager to bail you out if the market does poorly, so diversifying is extra important. If you own a stock index fund, make sure you also at least own a bond index fund.

6

Protecting the Downside: Insurance and Other Safeguards

IN THIS CHAPTER:
- Picking the right insurance
- Drafting a will, power of attorney, and health care surrogate
- Cutting the costs on these services

Now that your money is all set up and automatically growing toward your financial goals, absolutely nothing should come between you and a great financial life!

That's why your financial life needs the best possible insurance plans at the lowest possible cost. Here are the most important rules for picking insurance:

- Only buy from companies that are state licensed and that are among the financially strongest.
- Don't buy more than you need. Insurance is one of the most expensive financial services you can buy!

There are some other issues to consider when it comes to protecting the money you're accumulating. You'll need a power of attorney, a legal document that delegates financial decision-making to someone you trust, in case you become incapacitated. This can protect those you love from unnecessary legal expense. You also want a health care power of attorney or health care surrogate to make decisions about your health care if you can't. Plus a will is a necessity.

You certainly don't want all the money you've worked so hard to accumulate to go to the wrong people!

In this chapter, we'll give you some ideas on how to cover all these bases at the lowest possible cost.

TO DO LIST

- ❏ Investigate an insurance company's financial strength
- ❏ Check for an insurance company's state license
- ❏ Make sure you're thoroughly covered
- ❏ Set up a will, power of attorney, and health care power of attorney or health care surrogate
- ❏ Tell loved ones where important documents are located

Finding Financially Secure Companies

When you buy insurance, the U.S. government typically doesn't back your insurer's guarantee. So it's up to you to make certain that any company you consider is licensed to do business in your state. You can do this through your state insurance commissioner. Visit the website of the National Association of Insurance Commissioners (www.naic.org) for a list of state commissioner web addresses and phone numbers.

You also need to confirm that an insurance company you select is among the financially strongest. Unfortunately, determining a company's financial strength today isn't easy. Five different companies rate the financial strength of insurance companies, and each has a totally different system. Plus, not all companies are rated.

Here are the ratings companies:

- Moody's, www.moodys.com, 212-553-0300
- Standard & Poor's, www.standardandpoors.com, 212-438-2400
- A.M. Best Company, www.ambest.com, 908-439-2200

- TheStreet.com Ratings, www.TheStreet.com/ratings, 800-289-9222
- Fitch Ratings, www.fitchratings.com, 800-893-4824

TIP Good news: TheStreet.com Ratings, at its website, publishes lists of the nation's top-rated and lowest-rated insurers by category.

Be careful! Whereas a rating of B or lower means "vulnerable" by A.M. Best, it is considered "good" by TheStreet.com Ratings.

	Top Ratings	Vulnerable Ratings
A.M. Best	A++	B
Standard & Poor's	AAA	BB+
Moody's	Aaa	Ba1
Fitch	AAA	BB+
TheStreet.com	A+	D+

Source: Insurance Information Institute, New York

Other factors to consider are the size of a company and how long it's been in business. Also, it never hurts to check with the state insurance commissioner for complaints against a particular insurance company; use a search engine, like Google, to determine whether there have been problems, and check the company out at www.ripoffreport.com, www.consumeraffairs.com, and www.complaints.com.

TIP The National Association of Insurance Commissioners lists complaint information by insurance companies at its website, www.naic.org. Click on Consumers.

TO DO LIST

- ❏ Understand coverage offered by different types of health insurance
- ❏ Compare policies before buying
- ❏ Cut costs

Health Insurance

Unfortunately, health problems can derail efforts to reach your goals. Just one doctor visit today can run into the hundreds of dollars. As we wrote this, thank goodness, at least two states had adopted universal health insurance plans. But until more states or our federal government get on board with similar plans, it's up to you to weed through a maze of insurance options. Your objective: To find the lowest-cost plan with the broadest coverage. Plus, you want to be sure to pick a company that will be around when you need it.

Policy Types

There are several types of health insurance plans you can purchase, including indemnity policies, major medical, health maintenance organizations (HMOs), and preferred provider organizations (PPOs). Here's a short guide to these policy types:

- **Indemnity policy**—A basic policy that covers you for hospitalization and major medical problems. It usually does not cover doctor office visits. Covered hospitalization costs typically include doctor fees when you are in the hospital, surgery both in and out of the hospital, room and board, and nursing services. Also covered are x-rays, lab tests, blood transfusions, drugs, and medication. Typically, you're also covered for tests done outside the hospital.

- **Major medical coverage**—Picks up some of the tab that basic hospitalization insurance does not cover. Major medical pays for doctors, specialists, osteopaths, and chiropractors. The costs of outpatient treatment and drug and medical supplies, such as wheelchair rentals, respirators, and prosthetic devices, are also covered. Ambulance, x-rays, and lab expenses prescribed by the doctor often are covered.

> **TIP** What about a television and telephone in your semiprivate room? Unfortunately, you'll have to pay those out of your own pocket.

- **Health maintenance organization (HMO)**—Provides greater coverage, typically at a lower cost, than an indemnity policy. Once you pay your premiums, you can use an HMO's medical services either free or by making a small co-payment for each doctor visit. Co-payments often run from $20 to $25 depending on the plan. Many HMOs may require you to see a primary care physician. Depending on the plan, this doctor may be responsible for making referrals for any specialized care you might need.

- **Preferred provider organization (PPO)**—Works like an HMO but is more expensive because it lets you go to a doctor or hospital on the plan without obtaining a referral. You'll pay more, however, to go outside the PPO's network.

What to Examine Before Buying a Policy

Before you purchase a medical insurance plan, consider the following most critical points, besides financial strength:

- Make certain you are with a financially strong health insurance provider and that the insurance company is licensed to do business in your state. The financially strongest health insurance providers carry A+ to AAA ratings by Standard & Poor's and A+ to A++ ratings by A.M. Best.
- Look for an insurance policy that pays hospital bills from the first day you're hospitalized. Reason: Hospital stays are apt to be one of the most expensive services covered by health insurance. Yet, they usually run less than a week.
- If possible, aim for coverage that includes mental illness, elective medical procedures, and the purchase of generic drugs.
- Compare the maximum coverage your insurance will provide, and the maximum amount you'll be charged out of pocket.

Cut the Cost of Medical Insurance

Generally, the healthier you are and the younger you are, the less you'll pay for health insurance. If you're married and both spouses work, compare policies offered by both employers. It's best to go with the policy of the strongest company with the most benefits that charges the least out of pocket.

Here are some other ways to cut the cost of your health insurance:

- **Opt for higher deductibles**—A deductible is the amount you must pay out of your own pocket before the insurance company pays the bills. Most policies offer a choice of a $250 to at least a $2,000 deductible. After the deductible, the insurance company may pick up a percentage, say 80% of the tab, and leave the rest for you to cover—at least until you reach a maximum threshold for out-of-pocket expenses. To the extent that you can cover your own medical expenses and avoid getting sick, you can lower your cost.

> **TIP** With a new program, a Health Savings Account, you can save toward your deductible and medical expenses in a specially designated savings account that may be tax exempt. The downside is that these accounts require high deductibles of more than $1,000. So if you do get sick, you'll have to pick up a larger share of the tab. For more information visit www.treasury.gov.

- **Check for group rates**—If your employer fails to offer attractive benefits, shop other professional associations and shopping cooperatives for which you might get group rates. Sam's Club, a division of Wal-Mart, for example, has started offering small businesses a group health insurance plan. Many trade associations offer low rates for members. Also, check with your state insurance department for suggestions.
- **Consider COBRA**—If you've left a job, are unemployed, had your hours reduced, or have divorced or retired early, you might be covered by the Consolidated Omnibus Budget Reconciliation Act (COBRA). This act requires that group health plans sponsored by employers with at least 20 employees let employees buy health coverage at the employer's group rate for a specific period. For more information, visit www.dol.gov/dol/topic/health-plans/cobra.htm.

Disability Insurance

Try to get disability insurance—particularly if it's not among your employer's benefits. Your employer's worker's compensation insurance covers you only if you're injured on the job. There are two major federal programs under which you might qualify for disability benefits: Social Security and Supplemental Security Income. To get approved, you generally must be unable both to do work that you did before and to adjust to other work because of your medical condition. The disability also must be expected to last for at least one year or to result in death. Contrary to Social Security, Supplemental Security Income (SSI) is not dependent on income paid into the Social Security system. It covers food, clothing, and shelter. Besides helping the disabled, SSI also provides assistance to persons who are at least 65 years old or blind. For more information, visit www.ssa.gov or call 1-800-772-1213.

With private disability insurance, you should get a benefit of 50% to 60% of your gross income covered.

The cost of private disability coverage can be very expensive. A nonsmoker, age 35, with a gross income of $50,000 would pay about $1,500 a year for $25,000 in annual income coverage. You can lower the cost of the coverage by selecting a policy that does not cover the first 90 days that you are disabled.

When shopping for disability insurance coverage, it's important to consider several important criteria:

- Buy only from the financially strongest insurance companies, which carry ratings of at least A+ by A. M. Best, and AA by Standard & Poor's and Moody's.
- Compare policy premiums. You want the lowest-cost policy with the most extensive benefits.
- Your policy should be noncancelable and guaranteed renewable. This means the policy can't be changed or canceled without the policyholder's consent.
- Many policies give you the choice of collecting benefits for 2, 5, or 10 years or all the way to age 65 or longer. If possible, opt for the long term.
- Try to select a policy with a *cost-of-living adjustment*, which means that disability benefits rise as inflation increases but your premium stays the same.
- Try to select a policy with "residual value," which means you still can collect if you can work only part time.
- You also should have the option to increase your coverage as your income rises—despite any medical problems you may have.
- The policy should cover partial disability and disability caused by accidents.
- If possible, aim for a policy that covers you if you're unable to work in your specific field. Some policies may avoid covering you if you can work at any job.

> **CAUTION** If you get disability insurance through your employer, you'll likely have to pay income taxes on your benefits, which is not the case if you buy it on your own.

Online Advisor — To figure out how much disability insurance you should have, check out the disability insurance calculator at www.life-line.org/disabilitycalculator.

TO DO LIST

- ❏ Understand the major types of life insurance
- ❏ Learn to save money on term life insurance with a no-load company
- ❏ Find a professional to help you choose a policy

Life Insurance

If you plan to marry or already have a family, consider life insurance to provide income to your family when you are no longer around.

Life insurance is complex. It's often a good idea to have life insurance coverage that equals about five to eight times your current wages and income, to cover your loved ones. For example, if you make $50,000 per year, you should get $250,000 to $400,000 of life insurance coverage.

There are two common types of life insurance policies:

- **Term insurance**—With this, you get straight insurance protection. There is no savings component, which insurance agents often refer to as "cash value." Term insurance generally is the cheapest—at least for persons younger than age 50. This type of insurance provides protection for a specified period, although some policies are renewable. If you die while the policy is in effect, your beneficiaries collect the amount of insurance you've purchased. You can buy term insurance that is annually renewable or that is renewable every 5, 10, or even 20 years. The downside of term insurance: You generally can expect your cost to rise at renewal. Also, some insurance companies may require you to take a medical exam before letting you renew coverage. This can present a problem if you have a medical condition.
- **Whole life insurance**—This is a more permanent form of life insurance. Your monthly premiums fund a specific death benefit as well as a cash value savings account, which grows income tax–free. Insurance companies pass on excess earnings on whole life to policyholders in the form of dividends. Typically, dividends are used to buy more insurance. This can work to cut the number of years you must pay premiums. Need cash? You can obtain a low-rate loan on this type of policy. The downside: Whole life typically pays relatively low interest rates, set by the life insurance company, on your cash value. Frequently, you can do better investing on your own.

There are several types of whole life insurance. "Straight life" is most popular because you pay level premiums over the years.

Other types of policies provide more flexibility but may prove riskier. That's because the growth of your cash value is determined by current interest rates and investment returns in the financial markets. Among those types of policies are the following:

- **Universal life insurance**—Combines term insurance with a savings account that generally is higher yielding than that offered by whole life insurance. Your cash value grows income tax free and earns an interest rate, set by the insurance company.
- **Variable universal life**—Lets you invest in a selection of mutual funds income tax free. With variable universal life, you, rather than the life insurance company, decide when to buy and sell your investments.

With both types of universal life insurance, you needn't pay the same premiums every month. Have a bad month money-wise? You can cut your payment. Also, if the savings component of the insurance does well, you may never need to finish making your payments. The downside with this type of coverage: You can lose coverage completely if the investment portion of the account fails to generate enough income to cover the cost of your insurance. As with whole life, your cash value grows income tax free.

> **TIP** Life insurance proceeds that you get from the death of an insured person are not subject to federal income tax, according to the Internal Revenue Service.

LIFE INSURANCE RIDERS FOR SPECIAL SITUATIONS

You can use a "rider," at a cost of $50 to several hundred dollars annually, to fine-tune your insurance coverage. Here are the most frequently used riders and what they do:

- **Guaranteed insurability rider**—Lets you increase your insurance coverage without taking a medical exam or buying a new policy.
- **Disability income rider**—Tacks on some disability insurance coverage if you're unable to get it elsewhere.
- **Double indemnity or accidental death benefit**—If you die in an accident, your beneficiaries collect double the death benefit. Some policies also cover dismemberment, which means loss of limb.
- **Automatic premium loan provision**—Covers your premium payments in a financial emergency. The insurance company pays the premiums as a loan against the policy's cash value.
- **Waiver of premium**—Waives your monthly life insurance premiums if you get injured or become disabled. It is not designed, however, to be a substitute for disability insurance, which covers your income.
- **Family rider**—Lets you buy family term insurance with your whole life coverage.

Low-Load Companies

Do you prefer to get the cheapest term life insurance on your own, without an agent? Just as you can cut your cost on mutual funds by going to no-load fund companies directly, you also can cut your cost on life insurance by avoiding commissions. Unfortunately, there aren't as many to choose from. They include

- TIAA-CREF, www.tiaa-cref.org, 1-877-276-9429
- Ameritas Direct, www.ameritasdirect.com, 800-555-4655

Savvy Spending

If you go to a fee-only financial adviser, you also may get a break on costs. These advisers may sell low-load insurance, which charges lower commission. Or, they may charge you a fee to help you pick a low-load policy.

Getting Professional Help

If you decide to hire a professional to help you choose a life insurance policy, you want to get the best advice possible. Here are the different kinds of professional designations that persons who are licensed to sell insurance might have:

- **Certified Financial Planner (CFP)**—The CFP designation is awarded by the Certified Financial Planner Board of Standards, Inc. (CFP Board), Denver, Colorado. Candidates must have at least three years of financial planning–related experience and have successfully completed the CFP Board's initial and ongoing certification requirements. Learn more at www.cfp.net.

- **Chartered Life Underwriter (CLU)**—This designation signifies especially heavy training in life insurance. A CLU designation, coupled with a Chartered Financial Consultant (ChFC) designation, means the person also completed an eight-course financial planning curriculum. Both designations are issued by The American College, Bryn Mawr, Pennsylvania (www.theamericancollege.edu).

- **Personal Financial Specialist (PFS)**—This designation signifies heavy

> **TIP** The Consumer Federation of America has a life insurance evaluation service that's helpful once you have an "illustration," or description of how it works, from a life insurance company. Visit www.evaluatelife-insurance.org for more information.

> **CAUTION** If you ask an insurance company for a financial strength rating, beware that you could be quoted the one rating that portrays it in the best light. So make certain you get all company ratings.

training in accounting. It is given to Certified Public Accountants who pass a tough financial planning examination administered by the American Institute of Certified Public Accountants (www.aicpa.org).

Long-Term Care Insurance

Long-term care insurance nowadays generally pays for home health care, assisted living, and/or nursing home care. Although Medicare may provide limited coverage for skilled care, it typically does not cover simple loss of bodily function, which, unfortunately, is what happens to many of us as we age. Home health care, on the other hand, pays for a home health care aide, nurse, or other professional skilled care. Nursing home coverage is for hospital-setting skilled care.

Home health care, for a 24-hour aide, costs from $288 to $696 per day, depending on where you live, according to a MetLife study. That translates into $8,640 to $20,880 monthly. Meanwhile, four years in a nursing home can run at least $300,000. If you had to pay for this care, you could wipe out your life savings!

Unfortunately, the longer you wait to buy long-term care insurance, the more you're apt to pay monthly. Someone age 70 could pay as much as $3,600 per year for long-term care coverage, depending on the insurance company. On the other hand, get coverage in your 50s, and the monthly cost may be less than $1,200 a year or $100 per month. Of course, if you buy this when you're younger, you'll spend more for it over the long term.

So what should you do? For one thing, long-term care coverage at a younger age may be a more attractive bet for business owners, who can write off the cost on their income taxes. Also, there is something to be said for getting it while you're healthy. Otherwise, you may be unable to get it.

Just because you lock in a fee at a younger age doesn't mean your premiums won't rise. Generally, insurance companies raise fees for this coverage over time, but only for a class of persons with the same coverage. For example, the premium may be increased for all policyholders who have the same policy and who have reached their 72nd birthday.

> **CAUTION** If you stop paying your premiums on long-term care insurance, you could lose your coverage—no matter how long you've been paying! But some states have adopted laws to prevent this.

Here are some important policy features to consider, according to the Insurance Information Institute:

- Inflation protection that increases your coverage amount at 5% annually
- Guaranteed renewable policies, so that the company can't cancel you
- Waiver of premiums once you start collecting benefits
- Third-party notification in case you forget to pay a premium
- A provision that lets you keep a lesser amount of insurance in force if you let the policy lapse
- Restoration of benefits, which insures that your benefits are reinstated if you fail to go a specific period—often six months—without collecting

> **TIP** An increasing number of states—including California, Connecticut, Indiana, and New York—offer special long-term care programs and/or policies coupled with Medicaid benefits. It may pay to investigate these.

> **CAUTION** If you don't have long-term care insurance, or you have parents who could need nursing home care but lack long-term care insurance, make sure you see an elder law attorney. You can find one in your area through the National Academy of Elder Law Attorneys at www.naela.org. An elder law attorney with extra training may have a "CELA" designation.

Property Insurance

Insuring your property is just as important as insuring you family. Many of us have learned this lesson the hard way from the devastating hurricanes and earthquakes we've been having. Here, we talk about some of the most important types of property insurance and how to determine whether your coverage is adequate.

Automobile Insurance

Automobile insurance is a must. Here is what it typically includes:

- **Bodily injury coverage**—Covers injury to pedestrians and occupants of cars and damage to the property of others.
- **Medical payments coverage**—Covers medical bills incurred by you and/or the occupants of your car as a result of an auto accident.
- **Uninsured motorist coverage**—Covers you if you get injured or sustain damage to your car in an accident with someone who does not have insurance coverage.
- **Collision coverage**—Covers repairs to your car regardless of who or what caused the accident.

- **Comprehensive coverage**—Covers theft, vandalism, collision with animals, earthquakes, and floods.

> **TIP** If your car is at least five years old, you may be better off skipping collision coverage. But check the value of your car at www.kbb.com or www.edmunds.com to be sure.

Homeowner's Insurance

Homeowner's and renter's insurance cover your property against losses due to such sudden perils as fire, hurricane, hail, or lightning.

Your basic homeowner's policy covers

- The structure of your home
- Personal belongings
- Liability for lawsuits in case someone is injured on your property
- Living expenses in case you can't live in your home due to a disaster

With a standard homeowner's policy, your belongings usually are covered anywhere in the world. You even have up to $500 coverage for unauthorized use of your credit cards. However, you're probably limited to $1,000 to $2,000 of coverage for all jewelry and furs. Need more? Consider purchasing a jewelry rider.

Consider that "replacement cost" refers to the cost to replace your belongings at today's prices. Actual cost, by contrast, factors depreciation, and reimburses you for substantially less. Do you have a bank safe deposit box? Its contents, if damaged or stolen, are not likely insured either by your bank or the FDIC, so you might want to consider extra coverage for that. If you're in a hurricane or earthquake zone, be sure you have added coverage for those perils.

> **CAUTION** Be aware that homeowners policies do not cover flood insurance, which must be purchased from your insurance agent through the National Flood Insurance Program. Visit www.floodsmart.gov for more information. Even if you're not in a flood zone, experts warn that some flood zone maps were created before any development might have posed a flood risk.

> **TIP** Trees, plants, and shrubs are covered under standard homeowner's policies. But standard policies generally don't cover you for damage by wind or disease.

If you own a condo or co-op, you need to evaluate your association's master policy with regard to the common areas to make certain it covers all your needs.

Attorneys tell us that one of the greatest mistakes people make is to not purchase umbrella liability coverage, which generally costs some $300 annually for $1 million worth of coverage. This coverage kicks in if you're sued and you've exhausted the limits on your auto and homeowner's insurance policies.

> **TIP** Be sure to check whether you've qualified for any potential discounts. Here are some situations in which you may qualify for a discount: you have many types of insurance with one insurer; you have a burglar alarm system or hurricane shutters, in which case a homeowner's policy discount may be available; both you and your spouse purchase long-term care insurance.

To get umbrella liability coverage, you generally must purchase a minimum of $250,000 of liability on auto insurance and $300,000 on your homeowner's policy.

You Need a Will

A will is a legal document that determines who will manage your estate, who will get your property and belongings, and who will become guardian of your minor children when you die. If you die without a will, the state decides who gets what and who will take care of your children when you are not around.

Along with a will, it's a good idea to have your lawyer prepare a durable power of attorney and a living will. The *durable power of attorney* delegates to a person you specify the power to legally handle your business and financial affairs should you become disabled or incapacitated. If you fail to select a trusted person to exercise this power, no one will be able to access your bank account, securities, or any other property in your name without resorting to lengthy legal proceedings.

A *living will* lets you legally express your preference for continued health care should you later become incapacitated. A separate document, known as a designation of health care surrogate or health care power of attorney, names a trusted relative or spouse to make health care decisions for you in case you are physically or mentally disabled.

> **TIP** Keep your important documents and records in a fireproof safe deposit box in your home. But be sure family members have copies of them!

Summary

When evaluating any type of insurance company, the most important points to check are its financial strength and whether it has a state license.

Once you've determined a company is financially strong, compare prices and insurance benefits. You frequently can lower the cost of your insurance by raising a deductible and eliminating nonessential coverage. Also, check to see what special discounts the insurer provides.

Don't neglect setting up a will, to determine who gets your property when you die; a durable power of attorney, to determine who will manage your financial affairs if you become incapacitated; a health care power of attorney, to make determinations about your healthcare; and a living will, to specify your preference for continued health care should you later become incapacitated.

In the next chapter, we'll give you some ways to zip up your savings for retirement.

III

Supercharging Your Savings Plan

7	Saving for Retirement	95
8	How to Pay for Your Children's Education	109
9	Save by Choosing the Right Loans	121
10	Your Keys to the Good Life, Now and Later	137

7

Saving for Retirement

IN THIS CHAPTER:
- Understand how much you'll need to save
- Learn about your retirement income options
- Determine how well your retirement plan will work

Ah, the good life! Wouldn't you like to hang up the job, travel more, and maybe have a second home in Florida, Arizona, or Tahiti?

The earlier you start planning for these glorious days, the greater your chances of achieving your goals. This might sound impossible if you have cars that keep dying, a "money pit" home, and the cost of your children's college education to finance. But if you handle these financial obligations systematically, you can get there. If nothing else, you'll be much further ahead financially than you are now.

Speaking of systematic, please note we're putting this chapter on retirement planning ahead of what may be your other most expensive financial goal listed in Chapter 2: saving for your children's education. "That's strange," you might be thinking. "My children are going to need the money before I retire." We agree. But there's quite a bit of financial aid available for kids interested in going to college nowadays—some regardless of grades. So if you don't save as much as you'd like toward your children's education, your children probably still can get educated. Plus, they're young and have plenty of time to save their own money.

Neglect your own retirement, and who will take care of you? Your children? Believe that, and we've got a bridge to sell you in Brooklyn!

In this chapter, we'll show you how to start saving for your retirement, and direct you to all the programs that can help.

Determine What to Expect from Your Retirement Income Sources

Here's a rough breakdown of where your retirement income will likely come from when you retire:

- Social security: 30%
- Pension and investments: 70%

Let's look at these sources in more detail.

We told you in Chapter 1, "Examining Your Financial Condition," that the key to improving the bottom line of your financial life involves crunching numbers. With that in mind, the first step is to estimate how much you expect to get from Social Security and other sources of income for your retirement. You can get a rough estimate by using the calculators at www.ssa.gov. The Social Security Administration automatically mails a statement of estimated benefits to anyone over age 25 who has worked in Social Security–covered employment or self-employment. Unless you're already receiving Social Security, you should be getting this statement about three months before each birthday. When you get your statement in the mail, hold onto it! Lost it already? You can get another by calling (800-772-1213), visiting a local office, or through www.ssa.gov.

Today you can collect about 80% of your Social Security when you're 62 years old. Wait until your full retirement age, though, and you'll collect the full amount. Although the full retirement age formerly was 65 years old, those born after 1943 won't be able to take full Social Security pay until they hit age 66. Those born after 1960 won't be able to tap their full benefits until age 67.

Once you've nailed down how much you'll get from Social Security, the next step is to total how much you'll be able to collect from your other retirement savings accounts. These may include IRAs, 401(k)s, other company pensions, annuities, and life insurance. Plus, add in the reams of other investment income we hope you'll have.

Think you'll have enough? If not, Table 7.1 gives you an idea of what you'll have to sock away each month just to get an extra $100,000 at retirement—assuming the investment grows at an annual rate of 8%.

Table 7.1   What to Invest to Have $100,000 at Retirement

Years to Retirement	Monthly Investment
10	$575
15	$307
20	$219
30	$114

Wow! These monthly amounts may seem like a lot to put away to reach a single financial goal. But don't forget, you might already have some savings. Plus, you might be getting more Social Security down the road if your wages rise—that's assuming the U.S. government figures out how to fund it. Also, wait until the full retirement age, and you'll get even more Social Security benefits.

TO DO LIST

- ❏ Review your retirement plan options
- ❏ Learn about 401(k) savings
- ❏ Learn about IRAs
- ❏ Determine whether you need a Roth IRA

Your Retirement Plan Options

It's possible to give your efforts a major boost, courtesy of Uncle Sam, by choosing from a series of this good man's retirement plans. Unfortunately, many sound complicated. Uncle Sam sure hasn't made it easy for us to save. Plus, efforts were under way as we wrote this book to change retirement programs even further. So keep in mind that

> **NOTE** On certain retirement programs, including IRAs (individual retirement arrangements), simplified employee pensions (SEPs), and Roth IRAs, you have until April 15 of the following year to make your contribution.

whatever we tell you here could be changing by the time you read this, and be sure to check with your accountant. But once you understand the basics of retirement savings plans, pull the throttle and watch your money start taking off!

Retirement accounts can be great for one reason: The more of your monthly savings you can shelter in a retirement account, the less you're apt to pay in taxes. This can make your money grow even faster. Why not take advantage of as many of these programs as you can? Even though they sound complex, retirement plans really are no-brainers. The rules and the nature of the tax break you get depend on the plan you select. To qualify, you only have to do two things:

- Fill out the right paperwork—which any financial institution will be only too happy to give you.
- Obey the rules that apply to your specific retirement account.

We know there's a lot of misunderstanding out there about these programs. We've heard people talk about the IRA, one of the most popular types of retirement plans, as if it's just one investment. Not so. Exactly what you may invest in an IRA depends largely upon what the financial institution you select happens to offer. Your financial institution also sets the terms and fees of the retirement account. Set up a retirement account in a bank, for example, and it's possible your investment options include a lot of CDs. Set it up with a mutual fund company, and expect a great selection of mutual funds. Bottom line: It's up to you to pick the financial institution that has the investments you want for your retirement plan. It's also up to you to shop around for the best deals.

> **TIP** *Savvy Spending* Short on cash, have no pension plan at work, but know you'll be getting an income tax refund? Consider filing your income taxes as early as possible, and claim a deduction on an IRA, which we'll explain shortly, for the prior year. Then use your fatter refund check from Uncle Sam to fund it!

> **CAUTION** In Chapter 4, "Weighing the Pros and Cons of Simple Investment Options," we told you how to get an idea of what sort of investments you should own. Be sure that when you calculate the proportion of your money that should be in stocks, bonds, and cash, you always include your retirement account investments!

401(k)

401(k)s, also known as "salary reduction plans," are the most popular types of retirement plans, and are offered through employers. One reason they're so great is that you're allowed to contribute a percentage of your salary before you get your paycheck. This means that even though you pay income taxes on wages, you don't immediately on this particular contribution. Plus, your investment grows tax-deferred in your choice of whatever investments happen to be in your plan. On top of that, your employer may elect to contribute to your 401(k) as an employee benefit. What can be better than that? You also can borrow from a 401(k), often at attractive rates. Downsides: Any withdrawals you make before age 59 1/2, with certain exceptions that include hardships, may be subject to an IRS early distribution penalty of 10%. Plus, you'll pay income taxes on the withdrawal. Also, federal rules limit your contributions to this type of account. In 2006, those limits were a maximum $15,000 annually and an additional $5,000 annually if you're at least 50 years old. In 2007, that limit was to be indexed to inflation. The maximum an employer and employee together were allowed to contribute in 2006: $44,000. Unfortunately, you're required to start withdrawing from a 401(k) when you're 70 1/2 years old.

> **CAUTION** 401(k)s often require you to decide on an investment each year by a certain deadline. Miss that deadline and you could wind up earning a piddling amount on your hard-earned money.

IRAs

Individual retirement arrangements (or "individual retirement accounts") may let you take a full or partial deduction from your taxable income. If you have no other pension plan, or if you earn less than a certain amount annually, you might be able to save twice through an IRA: once by deducting your contribution on your income taxes, and again by deferring taxes on your earnings until you retire. Even if your contribution is not tax-deductible, you always have the advantage of tax deferment.

> **NOTE** The savings that tax deferment can bring are staggering. For example, if you're in the 28% tax bracket and you put $2,000 annually in a tax-deferred account for 20 years and earn 8% annually, you'd have at least $44,000 more in an IRA than you would by leaving it in a taxable account! Your IRA would grow to $98,846 compared with just $54,598 in a taxable investment. That's a big difference!

The bad news about IRAs: If you withdraw early, you owe income tax on the amount withdrawn, plus an additional 10% IRS penalty. There are some exceptions, which include withdrawing to pay for higher educational expenses or to buy, build, or rebuild a first home.

You must start withdrawing from your IRA account at age 70 1/2 according to special rules, based on your life expectancy. If you withdraw less than the minimum required amount, the IRS may assess a penalty equal to 50% of the amount of the minimum required distribution not taken.

CAUTION With an IRA, even if you deduct your contributions on your income taxes, you'll ultimately have to pay income taxes on your withdrawals. You'll also owe income taxes on your withdrawals from a 401(k).

In 2006 and 2007, you're allowed to contribute $4,000 annually to an IRA, or $5,000 if you're at least 50 years old. Those numbers were to rise in 2008 to $5,000 and $6,000, respectively. If you have another pension plan, for the year 2006, you still can, at the very least, take a partial income tax deduction for your contribution if your adjusted gross income is less than $60,000, or $85,000 for a married couple.

INVEST CAREFULLY IN A RETIREMENT PLAN

Don't put in a retirement plan money that you expect to need soon. Most have steep U.S. government–mandated penalties if you withdraw before age 59 1/2. Plus, you could owe taxes on the amount withdrawn. That's in addition to any penalties or termination fees your financial institution might also set.

On the other hand, because retirement accounts are designed to be long-term investments, a lot of financial institutions truly want your business. So always look for special incentives, such as better rates or low minimum required balances to open these accounts.

Roth IRA

A Roth IRA is the reverse of the traditional IRA, though limits on the amounts you're allowed to contribute are identical. Unlike with a traditional IRA, you can't deduct your contribution on your income taxes. However, your money in a Roth IRA grows income tax free and you can withdraw from it income tax free, which for many people can prove an even better deal. To withdraw tax free, you must have this investment at least five years and be at least 59 1/2 years old. Fail to meet these

TIP Starting in 2006, employers may let you designate some or all of your 401(k) contributions as Roth 401(k)s. Unlike with the typical 401(k), you get no upfront tax break through a salary reduction. But you would be able to withdraw your money income tax free provided you're at least 59 1/2 years old and have had the Roth-designated investments at least five years.

conditions, and you'll owe income taxes on the amount withdrawn. Among the exceptions to this rule is if you're withdrawing for first-time homebuyer expenses. Unlike with the traditional IRA, you don't have to make minimum withdrawals from a Roth IRA at age 70 ½. Have more than $110,000 in annual income, $160,000 for a married couple? In that case, at least in 2006, you probably can't contribute to a Roth IRA.

There are other types of retirement accounts for small businesses. Among those: a simplified employee pension (SEP), which is a type of traditional IRA but for small businesses, and a Savings Incentive Match Plan for Employees (SIMPLE). A SIMPLE plan is for employers with up to 100 employees who received at least $5,000 in compensation during the prior year.

Visit www.irs.gov and check out Publication 590, "Individual Retirement Arrangements (IRAs)," for more information on retirement plans. Uncertain whether you should invest in an IRA or a Roth IRA? Experts usually advise investing in the Roth IRA if you expect to be in a high tax bracket when you retire. Calculators at www.cch.com can help you figure out which to choose.

> **CAUTION** Leaving a job or want to change the financial institution that holds your retirement account? You can choose to have your plan transferred. Take possession of the proceeds, though, and you have 60 days to roll them over into another plan. Fail to meet that deadline, and you'll be forced to have 20% withheld for income taxes. Plus, you'll have to pay taxes on your retirement investments.

> **CAUTION** Annuities may have back-end surrender charges that can run as high as 6% in the first year if you withdraw your funds early, so be sure to review your contract carefully.

Annuities

If you've fully funded other retirement accounts and still need tax breaks, or if you'd like to guarantee yourself monthly income for life, an annuity could be the way to go. This is a contract with a life insurance company. You can either make periodic payments or deposit a lump sum into an account that grows tax deferred until you either withdraw funds or the contract ends, which may be up to age 85 or so. At that point, you have the option to withdraw all your money or receive periodic payments for life.

> **CAUTION** Regardless of the type of annuity you select, annuity guarantees are only as good as the insurance companies behind them. Be sure the company you choose has at least an A+ rating by A.M. Best. Also, if you need to qualify for Medicaid, the federal public assistance program that covers so many nursing home stays, some annuities may disqualify you from collecting Medicaid benefits.

If you take periodic payments, or "annuitize," the insurance company agrees to pay you the income for as long as you live. Beware that once you annuitize, you can't change your mind and cancel your contract!

If you withdraw from an annuity before you reach 59 1/2, you must pay the IRS a 10% penalty in addition to income taxes.

Annuities come in several shapes and sizes. Here are the most common:

- **Deferred fixed annuities**—This type of annuity pays interest as set by the insurance company for a specified period, after which the rate may change. Often, though, there is a minimum guaranteed interest rate.

- **Deferred variable annuities**—With this type of program, you do the investing, typically in a selection of stock and bond mutual funds. Your funds are placed in a separate account from the insurance company's pool of assets, and the investment risk falls on you. The idea: If you are willing to assume risk, you might be able to attain higher returns over the long term. Variable annuities have one other benefit: a death benefit guarantee. If you die, your beneficiaries—those who inherit the account—are guaranteed to receive either your original investment or the market value, whichever is greater. The downside is that annual charges can run more than 2%, according to Morningstar, Inc., Chicago. Plus, if your mutual funds perform poorly over the longer term, you might not have the kind of retirement kitty you expected.

NOTE With an immediate annuity, it is possible to arrange for loved ones to get some of your monthly payments through a "period certain contract." This means you get periodic income for life. But if you die within a specific time frame, such as 10 years, for example, your beneficiary receives the proceeds of your investment for the rest of that period. You also can arrange a "joint and survivor" pay-out option, so that periodic payments continue over the lifetimes of you and your spouse.

TIP With any deferred annuity, if you don't annuitize, withdrawals are taxed as ordinary income. This means the percentage of the income tax you pay depends on your income tax bracket. With immediate annuities, on the other hand, you pay income tax only on your earnings, not on your principal. So only about half of your periodic income from an immediate annuity is taxable.

TIP Some of the no-load mutual fund companies also offer no-load annuities—annuities without commissions—which also may have some of the lowest annual expenses.

- **Immediate annuities**—Already retired and need life-long income? With these, you can invest a lump sum and begin receiving payments immediately over the rest of your lifetime. In fact, deferred annuities can be converted into immediate annuities. Immediate annuities may be fixed or variable. Fixed payout rates are based, in part, on your life expectancy; variable payout rates are based on your investment performance and life expectancy. The biggest drawback is that once you sign the contract to annuitize, you can't change your mind. Unless you make other arrangements, the insurance company pockets your entire investment when you die.

ANNUITIES DIFFER SUBSTANTIALLY FROM IRAS

Contrary to a traditional IRA, only your earnings from the immediate annuity are subject to federal income taxes. By contrast, with a traditional IRA, you must pay income taxes on the full amount withdrawn—assuming you took an IRA deduction on your income taxes.

Also, with a deferred annuity, you stand to get some 15 years of extra tax-deferred earnings when compared with a traditional IRA. That's because you generally don't have to begin taking money out of an annuity until age 85. If you fail to start withdrawing your money from a traditional IRA by the time you reach age 70 1/2, you get hit with incredibly stiff IRS fines.

TO DO LIST

- ❏ Analyze potential retirement expenses
- ❏ Take advantage of as many tax breaks for retirement as possible
- ❏ Learn other ways to help fund and manage retirement expenses

Can You Retire?

To determine whether you'll finally be able to live the good life, you need to repeat the exercise we conducted in Chapter 1. Add up all the expenses you expect to incur in your retirement. The good news is that once you get to be 65, you're eligible to tap Medicare to cover your medical costs, so if you're paying for your own health insurance, you'll likely get off more cheaply with Medicare.

Then, add all the streams of income you expect to tap. Those include

- Assets you expect to get from your retirement accounts. We're going to leave it to the calculators to help you figure your IRA distributions.
- Defined benefit plans, which are plans that your employer might have set up and invested for you.
- Income you expect to get from non-tax-advantaged retirement accounts.
- Social Security

There are excellent online calculators that can help you with this task. Our favorites include www.smartmoney.com/retirement/planning and the retirement income and expense calculators at www.choosetosave.org/calculators.

Your list should look something like that shown in Table 7.2 (but with estimated income amounts filled in, of course).

Table 7.2 Annual Income from Retirement Assets

Asset	Income
IRA or pension	$
Annuity	$
Other savings	$
Real estate	$
Life insurance cash value	$
Trust assets	$
Social Security	$
Total	$

Next, use Table 7.3 or a similar worksheet to estimate your expenses during retirement. Table 7.3 gives you some rules of thumb about how much you likely will spend during retirement as a percentage of your income for some of the basics. You might use those figures or calculate your own estimated expenses.

Table 7.3 Expenses During Retirement

Expenses During Retirement	Estimated Percentage of Your Income	Expenses $
Food	15%	_____
Housing	30%	_____
Transportation	10%	_____
Insurance	Varies	_____
Entertainment	Varies	_____
Health care	Varies	_____
Taxes	Varies	_____
Debts	Varies	_____

Is your income greater than your expenses? If so, congrats! You can do it. If not, go back to Chapter 1 and figure out what more you can do to increase your income and cut your expenses. Your housing costs, including insurance, utilities, taxes, rent, and mortgage, should be 30% of your income or less. Figure that the cost of just about everything will rise about 3.5% per year—just in case.

Once you've analyzed this picture, you can figure out how well you're already doing and how much more you need to save. As you consider ways to cut your costs so that you can enjoy your life more, consider how you also might increase your investments.

WAYS TO TAP YOUR CASH

Today, most stock dividend yields are just 2% to 3%. When you retire, you can have those dividends, plus any capital gains sent to you every three months. However, that doesn't go very far.

You may also need to take systematic withdrawals from your investments. That means having your financial services company automatically sell a portion of your investments and send you a check each month. Most financial planners suggest that you take no more than about 3% to 5% annually in monthly distributions.

You can arrange for a mutual fund to send you a check monthly. Or you can have the money automatically deposited into your checking account or money market fund.

Remember, you'll probably owe taxes on some of the money you cash out.

Need More?

You also might be able to tap your home for cash when you retire through a *reverse mortgage*. Most reverse mortgage programs require that you be at least 62 years old. A reverse mortgage is actually a loan or credit line, based on the equity of your home. But you usually never have to pay this loan back until you move, sell the home, or die. The downside: These loans are riddled with steep fees and your heirs will be stuck paying back the loan from your estate. So make certain they've signed off on this plan. Also, you continue to own title to the property and still must pay for property taxes, insurance, and repairs.

Visit www.reverse.org for more information on reverse mortgages.

CAUTION Be careful! If you're collecting federal benefits on the basis of income or assets and putting draws from a reverse mortgage into a bank account, you could inadvertently be disqualified.

Other Ways to Retire

Still can't cut it when it comes to retiring?

Here are some other tips for trimming and managing the costs of your retirement:

- Find a cheaper way to live. If you live in a big home, downsize and move to a smaller one. Move to a lower-cost area of the country or, if rental income is high, consider renting your home and living in a lower-cost apartment.
- Cut medical expenses. Self-insure, by increasing the deductible on your health insurance policy to $2,500 or more. This also means staying in good health by exercising, eating well, and not smoking. You might also cut your medical expenses by living in another country.
- Work for a company that offers great retirement benefits.
- Take advantage of low-cost and free entertainment. Libraries and museums offer no- or low-cost entertainment. Consider free outdoor concerts. You can also cut costs by becoming more social. Get together with friends at your home or theirs, instead of paying for entertainment.
- Make the most of state and federal benefits to which you're entitled. Requirements for state, local, or federally subsidized housing may vary dramatically. Claim Social Security, supplemental security income, and Veterans Affairs (VA) benefits.
- Consider shared housing programs. Visit the National Shared Housing Resource Center at www.nationalsharedhousing.org for more information.

Also, check around for low-cost housing and loan programs or a reverse mortgage with state and local housing authorities as well as the Area Agency on Aging.

- Cut taxes as much as possible. Consider retiring to a state that has no state income taxes. At this writing, that includes Florida, Texas, Alaska, South Dakota, Washington, Wyoming, and Nevada.

> **TIP** As you near retirement, consider investing in more conservative or insured investments.

Summary

In this chapter, you learned how to best take advantage of retirement plans. Chief options to consider include 401(k) plans, which you may get on the job, traditional tax-deductible or tax-deferred IRAs and Roth IRAs, and annuities. Get the latest specifics on those and other programs at www.irs.gov. By saving as much as you can on taxes, more of your money can grow toward your retirement.

Add up your expenses and income streams to determine whether you have enough to retire. If not, other considerations may include downsizing your home, moving to a lower-cost area, or taking out a reverse mortgage.

In the next chapter, we'll tell you how to get your children through college.

8

How to Pay for Your Children's Education

IN THIS CHAPTER:

- Calculate the costs for college
- Determine how much you can save
- Review the best available tax breaks
- Learn the rules of college investing
- Track down scholarships and loans
- Find out what you can expect from financial aid

Saving for your children's college education may be one of your toughest challenges. But don't let it get you down. Your objectives: Make your children realize the importance of higher education, save as much as you possibly can for it, and help them check into scholarships and government loans. Another potential solution: lower-cost public schools or community colleges.

Evidence increasingly indicates that education is a key to both personal and financial success. Some four of five millionaires are college graduates, according to *The Millionaire Next Door* by Thomas J. Stanley, Ph.D., and William D. Danko, Ph.D. (Longstreet Press, 1996). So why not give your children positive reinforcement for concentrating on academics? Read with your children. Ask questions. Encourage good study habits. Children identify with their parents. Particularly, if you can let your children see how important their education is to you by adding it early to your list of financial goals, you're off and running to a great start. You've not only successfully established the goals of your own financial life, but you're starting to help them focus on theirs. Perfect priming for more great financial lives!

In this chapter, we'll offer up some ideas on how to pay for your children's education.

Getting Your Hands Around the Cost of College

College costs have been rising much more than the rate of inflation over the years. As we told you in Chapter 2, "Identifying Your Financial Goals," today you can expect to pay more than $12,000 per year at a state university, including tuition, fees, room and board—more than $48,000 over four years. A private school costs nearly $30,000 per year—$120,000 for four years.

If college costs increase at 5% annually—and some believe increases could be greater—expect four years of a state school to cost approximately $115,500 in 18 years. A private school would cost nearly $289,000 for four years. But don't forget, that's including room and board. You might be able to cut these costs if your child commutes.

Can you really afford this? Most can't. To pay the full amount of tuition, room, and board for your newborn child's college education at a state school, you'd need to save $336 monthly, assuming you could find an investment earning a 5% rate of return.

If you wanted Junior to go to a private school in 18 years, you'd need to put away a whopping $827 monthly, assuming an investment earned a 5% rate of return.

We already have you saving for your own retirement, so how much more can you possibly afford to put away? Probably not much. But there are a number of steps you can take to help cushion the blow.

> **TIP** Tuition at a community college runs about $2,000 annually. Assuming rates rise 5% annually, in 10 years, a community college would cost more than $3,258 annually; in 18 years, about $4,813 annually.

TO DO LIST

- ☐ Learn about prepaid tuition plans and investment accounts
- ☐ Understand how educational savings accounts work
- ☐ Learn the benefits and drawbacks of custodial accounts
- ☐ Learn about using IRAs and other tax-advantaged accounts for educational expenses

Step 1: Determine What You Can Save

Review your goals in Chapter 2 and estimate how much you can sock away each month. Rule of thumb: For every $84 per month you can save at 5% for 18 years, you'll be able to cover one year of tuition, fees, room, and board at a reasonably priced state college or university. To meet the cost of a four-year degree, you'd need to put away about $336 per month.

Have more than one child? Don't be discouraged. Over the years, the amount you can sock away could grow as your wages increase. Plus, we'll give you some tax-effective ways to save to help cut your cost.

Let's assume that you can't afford to invest $84 per month. That means you'd have to finance the rest through loans or scholarships.

Step 2: Examine Your Investment Options

This task can get a lot easier if you use one of the special savings vehicles created by Uncle Sam to help you get more mileage from your college savings through tax breaks. In Chapter 7, "Saving for Retirement," we showed you how much faster your money grows in an IRA if you defer taxes on it. But don't get confused; the plans we're going to tell you about are not single investments. Just like there are many types of retirement plans, there are several types of college savings plans. There can be a number of investment options within each type of plan. It is up to you to choose. Consider your child's college preferences, tax consequences, plan costs, influence on your ability to obtain financial aid, and available investment options.

Beware that all the investments we're about to describe may hurt your child's chances of qualifying for financial aid. Rules concerning this issue were changing and were expected to change even more, so if you think your child might need financial aid, be sure to check with your accountant and possibly a school financial aid administrator. You'll need to evaluate which program is least likely to hurt your child's chances of qualifying for financial aid, which provides the best tax benefits for you and, perhaps, whose name should be on certain accounts.

529 Plans

There are two types of 529 plans, named after the section of the Internal Revenue Code that created them: a prepaid tuition 529 plan and 529 investment account.

Under both programs, you get no federal income tax deduction for contributions. However, earnings are federally tax exempt provided that they are used for higher-education expenses. Most states also exempt earnings from state income tax. Certain states even let you deduct all or a part of your contribution from state income taxes! But be careful. State plans vary dramatically. Also, if your child decides not to go to college and you cash out, you could owe a steep penalty, typically at least 10% of earnings. You also may owe income tax on earnings.

Here are your 529 plan options:

- **Your state's 529 prepaid tuition plan**—These programs, sponsored by each state, let you lock into the price of tuition at in-state public universities and community colleges by making monthly payments or investing a lump sum. The good news: You typically don't have to worry about investment performance. You can transfer the benefits to another child if one child decides not to go to college and you even can get a refund if your child gets a scholarship. The downside: What if, after you save all that money, Junior decides to attend college in another state? State plans vary, but don't expect any in-state program to fully cover expenses of an out-of-state school.

- **Your state's college savings 529 plans**—These are state-sponsored investment accounts for which you often can invest as little as $100 and contribute more than $200,000. The types of investments available through these plans vary dramatically by state. So do costs. Investments may be mutual funds, CDs, or a professionally managed mix of securities. Expect to pay enrollment fees, annual maintenance fees, and/or fund expense fees. The good news: The person who makes the investment controls it until funds are withdrawn. The beneficiary does not have to limit college choices to a particular state. Plus, if the beneficiary doesn't attend college, the account can be transferred to another beneficiary. This is great if you have more than one child to educate. Downside: Unlike prepaid tuition programs, you have no guarantee that your investments will grow enough to cover the cost of college.

  > **CAUTION** (Online Advisor)
  > If you sign up for a 529 investment plan outside your state, you could wind up owing state income taxes on earnings—even though earnings may be exempt from federal income taxes. Check state tax policies at www.savingforcollege.com.

- **Independent 529 plan**—This plan is similar to a prepaid tuition plan, but lets you lock in tuition at a group of more than 250 participating private colleges. It's managed by TIAA-CREF, a major pension fund manager, and charges an annual asset management fee. Under the program, you purchase discounted certificates guaranteed to pay a fixed percentage of tuition at any of the participating schools. The downsides: Your child might not want to go to a participating college. In that case, you get a limited amount of your money back. Plus, withdrawals not used for qualified higher education are subject to income tax. For more information, visit www.independent529plan.org or call 888-718-7878.

> **CAUTION** The purchase of any 529 plan is no guarantee that your child will be accepted to college. Plus, the price of college tuition could fall—hurting returns on your investment in a prepaid tuition program or the independent 529 plan.

Coverdell Educational Savings Accounts

You get no federal income tax deduction when you participate in a Coverdell Educational Savings Account (ESA), but anyone is allowed to contribute up to $2,000 per year per child who is under 18. Withdrawals are tax free if used for qualified educational expenses, which (unlike the rules for 529 plans) may include elementary and secondary private school expenses. Your maximum allowable contribution is phased out if your adjusted gross income is between $95,000 and $110,000 in 2006, or $190,000 and $220,000 on a joint return.

> **CAUTION** In 2006, experts were warning that tax benefits of the Coverdell Educational IRA could expire in 2010.

Uniform Transfers to Minors Act and Uniform Gifts to Minors Act

With these special acts, which vary by state, you can set up a custodial account for your child by getting him or her a Social Security number. This way, you can arrange for income to be taxable at the very low child tax rate. The

> **CAUTION** The Uniform Transfers to Minors Act and Uniform Gifts to Minors Act are less attractive because much of the investment gains over $1,700 in 2006 may be taxable at the parents' tax rate until the child is at least 18 years old. Also, any time you give money, you must consider gift taxes, which are paid by the giver. In 2006, you're allowed to give $12,000 annually per person per child gift tax free. Give more, and you still might be able to offset the gift tax. Check with your accountant.

child gets the money at the age of majority, which generally is 18 or 21, depending on the state.

The downsides of this savings vehicle is that this account is irrevocable. Expect to be charged an annual maintenance fee. Meanwhile, if Junior prefers to splurge on a Porsche rather than go to college with your savings, too bad!

Other Tax-Advantaged Options

Here are a few other options you might consider for funding your child's education:

> **CAUTION** The penalty waiver for education expenses is not available on Roth IRAs.

- **IRAs**—We already described this type of retirement account in Chapter 7. Remember? Just in case you still need to tap it for higher-education expenses, you can. The IRS waives its 10% withdrawal penalty, normally charged if you withdraw from an IRA before age 59 1/2.
- **Series EE and Series I U.S. savings bonds**—We reviewed these in Chapter 5, "Creating a Plan that Works for You." Earnings might be tax free if used to finance higher education.

TO DO LIST
- ❏ Learn about the Hope Scholarship Credit
- ❏ Understand your eligibility for the Lifetime Learning Credit
- ❏ Deduct student loan interest from your taxes

Tax Breaks for College Savings

Online Advisor

Fortunately, Uncle Sam gives us a little more help in saving for education. But as usual with our good uncle, the rules are not easy to figure out, and keep changing. So visit www.irs.gov or check with your accountant for the latest. Basically, you're allowed to claim a credit on your income taxes based on any education expenses paid for you, your spouse, or your dependents—including your children.

The Hope Scholarship Credit

This provides for a credit on your tax bill of up to $1,500 per eligible student, but only for the first two years of post-secondary education. You can get a full credit for the first $1,000 of tuition and fees and 50% of the next $1,000. To qualify, the student must be pursuing an undergraduate degree or other recognized educational credential. The student must be enrolled at least half-time for a minimum of one academic period and the student must have no felony drug conviction.

> **TIP** Of the two types of credits discussed in this section, you can only claim one in any single year for each student.

> **CAUTION** There are income limits to qualify for either of these tax credits. Contribution phase-outs in 2006 began at $42,000, or $87,000 if you file a joint return.

The Lifetime Learning Credit

This credit provides up to a $2,000 annual credit per tax return—regardless of how many of your kids attend school. It's available for all years of post-secondary education as well as for courses to acquire or improve job skills. It's available for one or more courses—regardless of whether the student seeks a degree or other education credential. Unlike the Hope Scholarship Credit, the Lifetime Learning Credit can be claimed even with a felony drug conviction. Go figure!

> **NOTE** Tax credits are the cream of the crop. For each $1 tax "credit" you claim, you receive a direct $1 reduction in your income taxes. This is different from a "deduction," like the one you get for mortgage interest. For each $1 "deduction" you take, you only get your income taxes reduced by a fraction. But the limits on how much you're allowed to "deduct" on your income taxes usually are much greater than the amounts you can claim as tax credits.

Tax Deduction for Student Loan Interest

You might be able to deduct interest on student loans used to pay for higher-education expenses for you, your spouse, or a dependent. Check with your accountant, or visit www.irs.gov.

Rules for College Investing

We already told you in Chapter 4, "Weighing the Pros and Cons of Simple Investment Options," that if you're investing over the short term, you need to stay far away from stock-related investments. Over the long term, however, a good mix of stock investments may help boost your returns.

This definitely applies when you save for college. For a newborn infant, with 18 years to go before he or she is college bound, a mix of well-managed stock investments can be great! But as your child nears college age, be sure to keep your college-bound investments safe. Think CDs, low-risk bonds, and money funds.

Following are general rules for college-bound money you control:

- As a rule of thumb, never keep more than 75% in stocks or less than 25% in bonds. You need to make certain that market losses are cushioned.
- When you have at least 10 years to invest, keep most money in stocks or stock funds.
- When you have less than 10 years to invest, take money out of stocks and put more into short-term bonds, short-term bond funds, or money funds.
- If you're in a high tax bracket, consider investing the bond portion of your investments in tax-free municipal bonds or municipal bond funds. Also consider U.S. savings bonds.

Financial Aid

Now that you're saving for college, be sure you don't abandon efforts to get the most financial aid possible. As we told you earlier, the less you spend on one of the financial goals you set for yourself in Chapter 2, the more you have to apply to your other goals.

Too many parents think their kids won't qualify for scholarships, so they don't apply. Yet, there's a great deal of financial aid around that has nothing to do with need. So why not give it a shot?

Financial aid may come in three forms: scholarships, loans, and work. It's best to avoid loans if possible. First get all the free money you can! This takes some research because scholarship money often lies in places you might not consider. Take the scholarships we found at Juniata College, Huntington, Pennsylvania, for left-handed students. "How could such a scholarship come to be?" you ask. The college's husband-and-wife benefactors both were lefties!

Here's how to track down scholarships for your child:

- Fill out the free federal financial aid application at www.fafsa.ed.gov or call 800-433-3243. Apply extremely early! Grants available through this application run out fast! So even if you don't yet know the tax figures it requires, estimate.
- Check for scholarships at the financial aid office at the college to which your child is applying.
- Use the Internet. Websites to check include www.finaid.com, www.fastweb.com, and www.srnexpress.com.
- Don't assume that because one child got rejected that a second child you have going to college will. Financial aid formulas change if more than one child is in school.
- Check for scholarships offered by employers of family members, religious groups, community organizations, or trade groups. Be sure to check not only local branches, but also regional and national offices, which might have additional money available. Check foundations, religious organizations, civic groups, organizations related to your child's field of interest, retailers where you might shop, and labor unions.

> **CAUTION** Beware of scams. Some organizations that charge a fee provide you only with publicly available information.

- Check state education departments by visiting www.educationpolicy.org and scrolling all the way down to either State Education Agencies or State Agencies.
- To qualify for the most financial aid, keep assets in the parents' name and income in the child's name.
- Be sure to exclude your retirement assets on federal applications. They're not counted.
- Be careful. Some colleges will subtract any outside grants you get from college financial aid packages. So inquire in advance what the policy is for the financial aid office of the college your child is considering.

If You Must Borrow

There are various types of loans available for college. But be careful. Some are better than others. Here are some to consider:

- **Stafford loan**—Available to both undergraduate and graduate students. There are two types of Stafford loans. One, based on need, is the Federal Direct Loan, which is made directly from the U.S. government. With this program, Uncle Sam generally pays the interest. On an unsubsidized government-guaranteed loan, offered by private lenders through your school, your interest accrues and ultimately must be paid back.
- **PLUS loans**—These loans, made to parents rather than children, are not subsidized.
- **Private loans**—Salle Mae, www.salliemae.com, offers a signature loan to students, and its subsidiary, Nellie Mae at www.nelliemae.com, offers an EXCEL loan for parents.
- **TERI alternative loans**—The Education Resources Institute offers adjustable-rate loans for the full cost of college to parents or students. Go to www.teri.org for more information.

Other Ways to Get Your Children to College

Your child might be able to get a part-time job through the federal work study program, through a campus program, or simply by contacting businesses around campus.

If your child decides to serve in the military, the U.S. government should help fund college expenses in exchange for service. If your child would prefer to go to college first, he or she may participate in the Reserve Officers' Training Corps and qualify for merit-based scholarships in exchange for a commitment of three or four years.

Your child might be able to earn educational awards in exchange for community service. Visit www.learnandserve.org for more information. Scholarships and loans also are available through the Indian Health Service (www.ihs.gov).

Another option might be a home equity loan or credit line, secured by your home. Interest on these, when used to pay for college expenses, may be tax deductible. We'll discuss those further in the next chapter.

Summary

No doubt, it's important to get your children focused on education. It is an established key to personal and financial success. The first step is to figure out how much you'll need to save for your child's college education. Don't forget, you might be able to cut costs by focusing on public or community colleges.

Next, figure out whether any of the convoluted tax breaks that Uncle Sam gives you to save for college might help. Be sure to check for updates, because many rules were expected to change. Take advantage of the Hope Learning Credit or Lifetime Learning Credit on your income taxes for educational expenses. And if your child borrows for college, be sure to deduct interest on student loans.

Before borrowing, conduct an exhaustive hunt for scholarships that might be available. Next, try for the lowest-cost federally subsidized student loans.

In the next chapter, we'll tell you how to get the best possible deals on any loans you're forced to take.

9

Save by Choosing the Right Loans

IN THIS CHAPTER:
- Understand your loan objectives
- Get the best deal on credit cards
- Find a good car loan or lease
- Choose the right mortgages
- Learn about other types of loans
- Ditching these debts quickly

Sometimes, even with a great savings plan, you still must borrow. Perhaps you need a new car, and can't get to work without it. Or, maybe you want to buy a home with the objective of ultimately never having to pay rent again. In such cases, borrowing may make sense. But your objective is to get your loan at the lowest cost and get it behind you as quickly as possible.

Toward this goal, you always want to shop around for the lowest interest rates, lowest fees, and shortest term possible with payments you can afford. In this chapter, we'll tell you what to examine to find the best deals, and how to avoid many of the traps we've seen derail too many borrowers.

Your Loan Objectives

No matter what type of loan you seek, these are the objectives:

- Obtain the lowest available interest rate.
- Pay the least amount in fees.

- Keep the term as short as possible.
- Unless you expect to be paying off the loan very soon, it usually pays to stick with fixed interest rates. That way you always know what your terms and payments will be, and you can't get blindsided by rising interest rates.

> **NOTE** To compare apples to apples as much as possible, compare the annual percentage rate, or APR, which factors the annual interest rate and certain fees.

- Deal only with reliable lenders. Find out the name of the regulatory agency that oversees the lender you're considering, and check with that agency for complaints. For a list of regulatory agencies, see Appendix A, "References and Resources." Conduct an online search to see if anybody has written about any problems with your lender or initiated court actions against it. Check www.ripoffreport.com.
- Always negotiate with your lender on the terms of your loans. In some cases, lenders have discretion over rates and fees. Can't get fees waived? Ask if they will be refunded if you don't qualify.
- Watch for extra fees or services that you may not need but may be built into your loan, jacking up your balance.

> **CAUTION** Beware of lenders who woo you with low loan payments that have longer terms or potentially higher payments later on. Although you obviously would like a low monthly payment, such programs may cost you more interest in the long run.

The Scoop on Credit Cards

Although credit cards are financial life killers, it's not always a bad idea to have one. For one thing, it's tough to rent a car, purchase an airline ticket, or reserve a hotel room these days without a credit card. Credit cards provide the best protection if you buy something over the Internet. Also, if you're disciplined, it never hurts to borrow interest-free from your bank—even if it is for less than one month!

The other things we like about credit cards:

- You can't be held responsible for more than $50 if your card is lost or stolen.
- If there's a billing error, you can withhold payment of the charge pending an investigation. Simply write to the "billing inquiries" address on your card statement within 60 days after the first bill containing the error was mailed to you.

- If an item comes damaged or is of poor quality, you might be able to withhold payment by notifying your card issuer in writing. Just be sure you first try to resolve the issue with the merchant and don't pay the item off!

> **CAUTION** Debit cards, credit card convenience checks, and gift cards don't have as many federal consumer protections. Nor do business credit cards.

When exercising your federal consumer rights by notifying your lender, always write a letter to your lender, send it return receipt requested, and keep copies. Log the time, date, name, and title of any person you speak with concerning the issue.

Despite their benefits, credit cards also have ruined many a financial life. As a result, we urge you not to consider them unless you're certain you can pay off the full balance on time each month without accruing interest.

Always search for the best deals at www.cardweb.com and www.bankrate.com. Credit card issuers may reserve the right, after you apply, to offer you different terms based on your credit history. So be certain, before you use your credit card, that the terms are exactly what you ordered. Note ultra-high rates and fees, as well as annual fees, that may kick in under certain conditions, such as paying late, exceeding your credit line, or bouncing a check. You also might want to test out the credit card issuer's customer service line to see how long you have to wait for a live person.

Details to examine in the credit card agreement are the following:

- **The grace period or the number of interest-free days you have to pay your bill**—Your goal: at least 25 to 30 days.
- **Cash advance terms**—There typically is no grace period on cash advances. In addition, cash advances usually have much higher rates and fees than purchases.
- **Annual fee**—Try to avoid this entirely.
- **Guaranteed interest rate**—Check whether the interest rate is guaranteed and for how long.
- **Arbitration clauses**—With these clauses, already in most credit card agreements, you may be forfeiting your legal rights to have disputes heard in court if you have a problem.
- **Universal default clauses**—These clauses give the issuer the right to increase your rate or fees based on how you pay all your other loans.

- **Special fees or exorbitantly high interest rates on the remaining balance if you close your account**—You always want the option to switch to a better deal.
- **Rate application**—Particularly if you have a special introductory rate, make certain it applies to the type of transactions you intend to use. Often, attractive rates are limited to balance transfers. So you get no benefit if you make a purchase. The opposite may also be true.
- **Other special fees**—Watch for special fees due to balance transfers and convenience checks.
- **Interest application**—Monitor how interest charges are applied to pay off your balance. Often, attractive teaser rates are the last to be applied. That means you're stuck paying the highest rates for the longest periods.

ESTABLISHING OR REBUILDING YOUR CREDIT RECORD

Follow these tips to build (or rebuild) a healthy credit record:

- Apply for an in-store retail credit card. These cards often are the easiest type of unsecured credit card to get.
- Obtain a secured credit card. The credit card loan is secured against a savings account or perhaps a CD. You can find a list of secured credit cards at www.bankrate.com or www.cardweb.com.
- Confirm in advance that the card issuer will report your payments to the credit bureau. If not, shop around.
- Always pay your card on time. After a while, you can get an unsecured card.
- If you're new to the United States, ask about special mortgage or credit programs that are available to immigrants.
- Married women with no work history can become an authorized user on a spouse's credit card. That's a way to build a good payment history.

Understanding Car Loans and Leases

Unfortunately, in most areas it's tough to have a job without a car. The problem: A car is a losing proposition. Unlike with a home, it's tough to get most of your money back if you ever sell it. Plus, unlike mortgage interest, car loan interest is not tax deductible.

Online Advisor: Don't buy a car before visiting Edmunds, www.edmunds.com; Kelley Blue Book, www.kbb.com; and the website of the National Automobile Dealers Association, www.nadaguides.org. Don't set foot into a car dealership without knowing in advance the type of car you want and the going cost, which these websites provide. Expect to pay a higher interest rate for a used-car loan than for a new-car loan. Also check car loan interest rates online. Historically, nonprofit credit unions have tended to have among the lowest car loan rates. To get a car loan from a credit union, though, you'll be required to open a savings account or "share account."

Savvy Spending: Leases, many consumer attorneys believe, are the worst deals when it comes to car financing, and should be avoided. With a car lease, or any other type of lease, you never own the item. Yet, you may have to pay upfront costs, such as one month's payment, a security deposit, a down payment and taxes, registration, and other fees.

The good things about car leases:
- Monthly payments are lower than they are with a car loan, so you may be able to afford to drive a fancier car.
- If you use the car for business, you can write off the cost of the lease on your taxes.

The bad things about car leases:
- When a lease term expires, you don't have a car to trade in. You can turn the car into the dealer or buy it at a higher price than you might pay for a similar make and model car elsewhere.
- Break your lease early, and expect to be responsible for killer termination penalties.
- Most leases restrict the number of miles you can drive annually. Estimate wrong on your anticipated annual mileage, and you'll likely pay significantly higher per-mile costs at the end of your lease. You'll also owe added costs for excess wear and tear.

If you must lease, compare the following:
- The agreed-upon value of the vehicle. You want it as low as possible.
- Upfront payments.
- The length of the lease.
- The monthly lease payment.

- Any end-of-lease fees.
- Mileage allowances and per-mile charges for excess miles.
- The residual value or price at which you can purchase it at the end of the lease.
- Whether it includes "gap" coverage. This covers the difference between what you owe on your car lease and what your car insurance covers if the car is lost or stolen. The difference can be significant.

> **CAUTION** With a lease, you'll likely be required to have higher insurance coverage limits than you'd need if you were to buy a car.

TO DO LIST

- ❏ Find out about loan fees.
- ❏ Compare mortgage types.
- ❏ Get information on special mortgage programs.

Picking a Mortgage

Mortgages are among the most complex loan instruments there are. So it's extremely tough to ferret out information you need. First, you need to determine whether you want a fixed-rate mortgage or adjustable-rate mortgage, or whether you are interested in pursuing another special type of mortgage. For any mortgage, you need to evaluate the fees.

Checking Out Loan Upfront Costs and Fees

In addition to interest rates and fees, there are two mortgage wrinkles you need to know about:

- **Closing costs**—These are a slew of fees that you pay at closing. Some may be negotiable. So raise questions about each one you don't understand. Plus, if your lender is using a particular vendor for, say, inspections or title insurance, you might check around to see if you can find a cheaper option.
- **Points**—This term is another way of expressing fees. One point is equal to one percent of the loan amount. To find out the cost of a point, convert it to a decimal—that is, one point equals .01—and multiply it by the amount you're borrowing. On a $200,000 mortgage, one point would be equal to $200,000 × .01, or $2,000.

SHOULD YOU TAKE UPFRONT POINTS OR A HIGHER LOAN RATE?

Lenders may offer you a choice: pay points up front or pay a higher loan interest rate instead. Generally, one point is equal to between one-eighth of one percent and one-quarter of one percent added onto your mortgage interest rate.

Keep in mind that adding points and fees to your balance may dramatically add to your loan cost. You're paying interest on a higher balance over a potentially long period.

The good news: When you apply for a loan to purchase a home, upfront points are income tax deductible. If you're refinancing, points are income tax deductible over the life of the loan.

We've actually had lenders tell us that there are "no closing costs" or upfront fees on a mortgage. When we probed further, we learned there definitely were fees for such items as an appraisal, title insurance, and survey! Funny. Some lenders just don't consider those fees. So when you shop for a mortgage, be particularly skeptical.

> **TIP** It's rare for lenders to waive appraisal fees and title insurance fees, as well as other fees they usually pay to third parties. So if you're told there are no fees, make certain these particular costs are not simply being added to your loan balance, which can prove more costly in the long run.

Choosing a Mortgage Type

The two most basic types of mortgage are fixed rate and adjustable rate. An adjustable-rate mortgage may be attractive if the initial rate is significantly lower than the rate you'd pay for a 30-year fixed-rate mortgage and you don't expect to be in the house long. A great place to check out this information is www.hsh.com.

If you are considering an adjustable-rate mortgage, you need to ask some important questions before you choose: Does the adjustable-rate mortgage have a payment cap rather than a rate cap? Is the adjustable-rate mortgage an option ARM mortgage?

In these scenarios, you're probably signing on to a loan that could have *negative amortization*, which means your principal can rise even though you're making monthly payments. This really hurts when rates increase—particularly if you need to sell your home and prices have declined. Even though your monthly payments may be limited, an increasing amount of interest still may be tacked on to your loan balance. If your monthly payments don't cover it, you could wind up owing more than your home is worth!

Also, beware of mortgage contracts that let the lender recast your entire loan. Some contracts do this, say, at the end of 5 or 10 years, and/or once you owe 110% of your loan balance. If this happens, your monthly payments and/or balance could increase dramatically!

> **CAUTION** Don't buy loan officer arguments that real estate always appreciates so it won't matter in the end how your rate or amortization changes. We've already seen lengthy periods where home prices have stagnated and even declined.

If you do consider any adjustable-rate mortgage, always evaluate the following:

- **Interest rate caps and rate floors**—Make certain your lender computes what your maximum monthly payment will be once your rate hits the lifetime rate cap. Always ask for the worst-case scenario. When rates were dropping, and adjustable-rate mortgages truly were a good deal for many borrowers, rate floors prevented them from receiving the full benefit of the rate decline.
- **Frequency of rate adjustments**—With a one-year adjustable-rate mortgage, the interest rate adjusts annually. With a six-month adjustable-rate mortgage, the interest rate adjusts every six months—even though monthly payments may adjust annually. The more frequent the rate adjustment, the faster you can expect to accrue interest charges in a rising rate environment.

Other types of mortgages include the following:

- **Hybrid mortgages**—These mortgages have a fixed rate for a certain number of years. You might be able to select from a three-, five-, or seven-year period, for example. After the fixed-rate period, the loan automatically converts into an adjustable-rate mortgage for the remaining term. These mortgages may be attractive when 30-year fixed-rate mortgage rates are significantly higher than the fixed-rate period of a hybrid mortgage, yet you desperately want a home. They may provide more rate stability than an adjustable-rate mortgage. Consider these when you think you'll be selling your home or paying the mortgage off by the time the fixed-rate period ends.

- **Balloon mortgages**—These mortgages, which may be either fixed rate or adjustable rate, typically have significantly lower monthly payments than a standard 30-year fixed-rate mortgage. Usually, payments are all or mostly interest, which may be tax deductible. No principal or very little is ever paid off. At the end of the term, which frequently is significantly less than the standard 30-year term, you owe a whopping payment that represents either the bulk or full principal of the mortgage. Sometimes lenders agree in advance to let you refinance this "balloon" on their terms. But expect either the monthly payments to skyrocket or your term to increase. These loans can prove attractive if you know you'll be selling your home before the balloon payment is due. Example: You bought the house due to a job transfer and likely will be relocated again.

> **CAUTION** Consider balloon mortgages only if you're fairly certain you won't be in your home or carry the mortgage longer than the term of the low monthly payments.

- **Option mortgages**—The name of these mortgages, which can have fixed rates or adjustable rates, refers to the fact that they offer you a selection of payment options. One selection typically is interest only. Another has even lower monthly payments that often result in negative amortization. This loan can be very risky but can be attractive, say, for an investor, who might want to pay less in certain months while the property is unrented.
- **40-year or 50-year mortgages**—The standard mortgage term is 30 years. Increase the term, and you'll have lower monthly payments, but you'll owe more interest in the long run.
- **15-year fixed-rate mortgages**—Rates typically are lower with a 15-year fixed-rate mortgage than with a 30-year fixed-rate mortgage. But even if you refinance and lower your rate, expect your payments to be higher unless rates drop very significantly.

When evaluating any mortgage, always

- Consider that your monthly mortgage payment likely also will include an extra amount in an "escrow account," so that your lender can cover insurance and property taxes. This can increase your monthly payment by about one-third. Some lenders may offer to waive the requirement for this account and let you pay insurance and property taxes yourself, often in exchange for added fees or points.

- When applying for a mortgage, consider locking in your rate in case interest rates rise. Some lenders charge a higher interest rate for this privilege, or there may be an extra fee. But without a lock-in, you're unprotected if rates rise before you close on your loan. If you're dealing with a mortgage broker, who may be selling a loan offered by another lender, try to get a copy of the "loan commitment letter" from the actual lender. There have been cases of mortgage brokers going out of business and borrowers being left out in the cold. Keep evidence of any extra payment or your agreement for the lock-in period.
- Consider any prepayment penalties. Some lenders may charge a lower interest rate in exchange for a prepayment penalty. Terms of prepayment penalties may vary. Some, for example, kick in only if you refinance.
- Make certain you hound your loan officer to ensure that each step of the loan process is followed quickly. After all, you'll need to have inspections, surveys, and title insurance well in time for closing. It's very common for lenders to drag their feet when they get busy—particularly if you're refinancing a loan rather than buying a home.
- File a written complaint fast with your lender's regulatory agency if the process gets delayed!
- Make certain you obtain a "satisfaction of mortgage" as proof once you finally pay off your mortgage.

Finding Information on Special Mortgage Programs

Can't afford a standard 20% down payment? In that case, you'll probably be required to purchase private mortgage insurance (PMI) or take out a second loan to cover part of your down payment. Make certain you fully understand the costs and terms of these options. Find out how long you must pay private mortgage insurance. You want to get rid of this added cost as soon as possible.

You might be able to qualify for a low down-payment mortgage program through an FHA loan. For more information, visit www.fha.gov.

Also, check with city, county, and state housing agencies in your area. If you're a veteran, you might qualify for a loan from the Department of Veterans' Affairs. With this type of loan, you needn't make a down payment or pay private mortgage insurance, but lenders can charge whatever they wish, so they may not always be the best deals. Visit www.homeloans.va.gov for more information.

Cities and other employers may offer down payment assistance as job benefits. For special programs in your area, visit the National Council of State Housing Agencies at www.ncsha.org and click on About NCSHA to find out your area agencies.

> **TIP** See the mortgage shopping worksheet in Appendix C.

Home Equity Loans and Lines

Home equity loan programs are very similar to mortgages. With a *home equity loan*, you're borrowing a fixed amount and paying it back over a specific period—much like a car loan. A *home equity credit line*, on the other hand, works like a credit card. You have a credit limit, based on the value of your home. Much like a credit card, you can access a home equity credit line at any time either by checks or a credit card. These programs may have either fixed or variable rates.

> **CAUTION** Although these loans are treated like consumer loans, the lender can take your home if you fail to make payments.

We've often heard financial advisors or bankers suggest that you buy a car with a home equity loan so that you can deduct interest on your income taxes. This may be a viable strategy—as long as you fully understand that if you don't pay, it's possible to lose both your car and your home!

Home equity lines also are hyped as a way to consolidate debts. However, consumer debt counselors warn that if you do this, you're turning unsecured debt into secured debt and putting your home on the line.

Too many people, they warn, take out a home equity line, and start racking up new debt, often on frivolous purchases. If you lack self-discipline, avoid these loans like the plague.

Other Low-Cost Ways to Borrow

If you must borrow, here are some other loans to consider:

- **Collateralized bank loan**—You could use a bank certificate of deposit or savings account as collateral for your loan. If you borrow the money from the

> **NOTE** You need to be especially careful to check all fees associated with home equity loans or lines of credit. No closing costs on a home equity credit line? Check for termination fees, non-usage fees, annual fees, and/or fees if you fail to draw down a specific amount. As with mortgages, you also must watch for interest-only payments, which means you could find your entire loan due after 5 or 10 years or be saddled with much higher monthly payments.

bank, expect to pay two to three percentage points above the prime rate for the loan. The drawbacks: Your loan interest isn't tax deductible. If you can't pay back your loan, the bank takes your collateral.

- **Borrow from your company pension**—Employees can borrow against the vested balance up to a maximum of $50,000 at low rates. In most cases the loan must be paid back within five years. The loan interest isn't tax deductible. Most companies automatically deduct from your weekly paycheck to pay back the loan. Drawback: Fail to pay it back within the required time frame, and you could be taxed twice by Uncle Sam—once on your income and again for withdrawing early.

- **Borrow against the cash value of your life insurance policy**—In many cases, insurance policy loans charge very low or zero interest rates. Drawback: Your death benefit coverage will be reduced by the amount of your policy loan.

- **Margin loan**—You might be able to borrow at a lower rate on your securities. But if the value of your securities drops below a certain level, it may trigger a "margin call." You'll be forced to pony up the cash to cover your loan. Fail to pay and you can lose your assets.

Beware When You Borrow Money

Whenever you borrow money for a large item like a house or a car, it means big money for a lender. Here are some rules to avoid being hoodwinked:

- Avoid as many extra insurance policies sold with loans as possible. Particularly if you're financing the cost into your loan balance, you're generally paying way too much. Often, it's cheaper to add coverage to a homeowner's or renter's policy instead.

- When you buy a home, you could be rejected for a home loan if the appraisal comes out lower than the amount you're borrowing. So don't buy a home without obtaining a "comparative market analysis." This report, generally available for free from your real estate agent, gives you the prices of

> **TIP** You can get a free comparative market analysis of a home you are considering at www.zillow.com. You also might be able to get sales prices of homes online through county or local government tax appraisers. But beware that online data might not always be the most current.

similar homes in the area. It helps provide a key to determining how much to offer for a home.

- If possible, avoid extending the term of your loan when you refinance. That adds to your cost.
- If possible, avoid finance companies. They typically charge more than banks, savings institutions, and credit unions.
- Unless it's an emergency, consider avoiding cash-out refinancing in which you borrow more than you already owed. These can sink you further into debt.
- If there's a chance you may declare bankruptcy, consult with an attorney before taking out a loan. You especially don't want to turn installment debt into secured debt, with assets creditors can take!

> **CAUTION** Avoid payday loans (which generally charge steep fees per amount borrowed) and tax refund anticipation loans. These are costly. The IRS offers a "Free File" program to those who earn less than $50,000 annually. You can get a tax refund direct deposited to your bank account within two weeks. Bank overdraft protection may provide a less costly option to payday loans. Military personnel may turn to Air Force Aid Society, Army Emergency Relief, Coast Guard Mutual Assistance, Navy-Marine Corps Relief Society, and the Armed Forces Relief Trust for financial help.

Eliminating Debt from Your Financial Life

Now that we've given you the straight scoop on several types of loans, here are some quick tips to get debt—and its accompanying costs—out of your life.

Refinance Your Home

Be sure to refinance your home only if it makes sense! Refinancing typically comes with upfront costs.

Refinance only if you plan to stay in your home for enough years to recoup your closing costs through your savings on monthly payments. Don't know, for sure, how long you'll be in the home? The general rule of thumb is to make sure you can recoup your upfront costs within two years.

Online Advisor

There are a number of online calculators to help you determine this. Check out

- www.bankrate.com
- cgi.money.cnn.com/tools/cutmortgage/cutmortgage.html
- www.hsh.com
- www.dinkytown.net

Before you refinance, ask your existing mortgage lender for a lower rate. This can save you quite a bit on closing costs because your lender already has much documentation on file.

Because car loans have much shorter terms, it may not make as much sense to refinance those—unless you have no upfront fees and you're not extending your term.

Prepay Your Mortgage

Of course, you can't afford to prepay the full amount on a large loan. But if possible, why not take advantage of the fact that most of your interest is charged in the first few years of your mortgage? First, check to see whether your mortgage has a prepayment penalty.

If not, here's what to do. Get an amortization schedule from your lender. Or, print one out for free at one of these calculators:

- www.hsh.com
- www.bankrate.com

Say you have a $200,000 30-year fixed-rate mortgage at an interest rate of 6%. Your monthly payment is $1,199.10, according to a calculator at www.hsh.com. Make that payment. In the same envelope, stick a second check for the following month's principal, $200.10, excluding interest. Make certain you notify your lender in writing to apply the $200.10 to pay down your mortgage principal. Cross the first two monthly payments off your amortization schedule, and repeat this process every month. You'll pay your mortgage off much sooner and save a whole lot of interest!

Consider a Biweekly Mortgage

Be careful with this tactic. This is an area ripe for rip-offs. A lot of lenders and independent companies will offer to convert your loan to a biweekly mortgage for an exorbitant fee. Frequently, you're buying use of a software program.

But you may be able to do this yourself on your loan if your lender cooperates. Simply make the same monthly payment, but pay it in two installments—one on the fifteenth of the month and the second on the thirtieth. In fact, see if you can have the amount automatically deducted at those times. By doing this, you should be able to slash your term on a 30-year fixed-rate mortgage to about 18 years, saving tons of interest!

Some lenders charge a fee to do this. Others are happy to get the loan off the books faster, and will offer it as a free service. Some lenders require you to open a checking account at their institution if you want to make biweekly payments.

If you run into obstacles with this strategy, just make one extra payment annually. Add a note instructing your lender to apply it to your principal. You generally can accomplish the same objective: getting out of debt faster!

Summary

Okay, in certain cases you need loans. But if you must borrow, it is best to aim for loans with the lowest rates, lowest fees, and shortest terms, even though lenders will try to get you to focus on the size of your monthly payments.

Avoid financing extra fees into your loan balance. You'll ultimately increase the interest you pay. Also avoid financing extra insurance policies you may not need.

Once you've qualified for the loan you're seeking, take steps to pay it down as fast as possible!

In the final chapter, we'll discuss how to keep your financial life heading on the right track.

10

Your Keys to the Good Life, Now and Later

IN THIS CHAPTER:
- Know your income and spending patterns
- Evaluate your insurance coverage
- Revisit your investments
- Check your tax status
- Review your estate plan
- Sit back and enjoy your financial stability

By now, we suspect you've made some great progress, and your financial ship is sailing on an even keel. If not, at least you're moving in the right direction. But that doesn't give you a license to revert to your old ways and ignore your precious financial life again.

Like any good CEO, you need to keep your financial life positioned on a positive track. This requires periodic evaluations.

Circumstances surrounding your financial situation can change in a flash in so many ways. You could lose your job. You could get promoted. You could have another child. There may be new investment options. Or, perhaps, state or federal regulations governing your investments may change. Any one of these transitions likely will require some new action.

In this chapter, we show you how to periodically examine your financial life so that you spot important issues that require change. Then, you can fine-tune the progress you've made so far.

Evaluate Your Income and Spending

In Chapter 1, "Examining Your Financial Condition," and Chapter 2, "Identifying Your Financial Goals," you succeeded in nailing down where you are and where you're going financially. But it's important that you conduct these exercises at least annually. After all, you might not have taken that vacation you were expecting to take in 2005. Keep the cash in a checking account, and watch it disappear! Wouldn't it be better to put all the money you've saved on that extravaganza toward financing your child's college education?

That is just one example of why it can pay off handsomely to make an annual habit of reviewing your income, expenses, and goals. Make adjustments in your plans, make certain your spending is on track, and put away as much money as you need to enhance the quality of your financial life.

Here's a checklist to help you decide if adjustments are in order:

___ **Log expenses**—Each year, write down expenses listed in your checkbook register and on your credit card and savings account statements. Add in cash you spent. Figure your average monthly expenses in each category. Write down how much you are spending monthly on food, clothing, transportation, housing, utilities, health care, and entertainment. Compare it with the previous year's. Has some of your spending gotten out of line? If so, examine whether there's anything else you can cut to compensate.

Example: This year, we experienced large increases in our electricity and water bills. In addition, a restaurant to which we went for Saturday breakfast raised prices dramatically. As a result, we agreed to stop going out for breakfast on Saturdays. Instead, we've adopted the equally pleasurable, but significantly less costly experience of sipping mimosas and eating Saturday brunch outside by our swimming pool. Not so terrible. With a little vigilance, you, too, can conduct a similar exercise. Then, watch your net worth grow!

___ **Examine your income**—Every year, examine your sources of income. Did you get a raise at work? Or did you get a pay cut? Are you getting investment income? Did you get an inheritance? Did you make some extra income from the sale of an asset? If your income is lower than last year, you need to examine new ways to raise it. Perhaps you need to ask your employer for a raise. Or, maybe it's time to change companies. If you've obtained more money, evaluate how much more you can put toward your financial goals. Or, perhaps it's time to finally splurge on some new, short-term fun objectives!

___ **Calculate expenses**—Subtract your monthly expenses from your monthly income to determine where your financial life stands. Is your financial life making a profit? Or, is it losing money? Brainstorm on any additional ways you or your family might bring in extra cash.

___ **Revisit goals**—Reevaluate your goals and make necessary adjustments. Perhaps this year you suddenly have a new bundle of joy. In that case, you'll have to add new goals, such as saving for college. Plus, you may have to add in extra expenses you'll need for clothes, food, and health care for Junior!

___ **Evaluate your debts**—Is the amount you owe rising or falling? Have interest rates dropped or increased? Might you be able to get a lower-rate credit card? Perhaps you can refinance your mortgage. If your debt is increasing, evaluate what steps you can take to wipe it out. Might you take a temporary part-time job? Perhaps you can double up on payments.

Evaluate Your Insurance Coverage

Insurance can be one of your greatest costs, so it pays to evaluate it annually. Review Chapter 6, "Protecting the Downside: Insurance and Other Safeguards," for more specifics. But you'll definitely want to ensure that policy terms and regulations, as well as your own needs, haven't changed. Are you on the best plans possible at the least possible cost? Be sure that each insurance company you use still is highly rated. Are beneficiaries correct? Are there any new provisions available that are important? We've heard of people who had gotten divorced, yet forgot to update the beneficiaries on their life insurance policies. As a result, proceeds inadvertently went to ex-spouses!

Here's a yearly checklist to make sure your insurance coverage is adequate:

___ **Life insurance**—Do you have adequate life insurance? If you've had another child this year, you may need more. You may also need more if your assets have grown so much that you'll owe estate taxes. Have you married, divorced, or added children to the family? In that case you may need more insurance. You also may need to change beneficiaries.

___ **Disability insurance**—Do you have enough disability insurance? Again, if you're making more money, you may need more coverage.

___ **Auto and homeowner's coverage**—You might need more coverage if you live in an accident-prone area or are more vulnerable to tornadoes, earthquakes, hurricanes, or floods. You might want to consider getting umbrella insurance. Got a new diamond ring? You might also need to add personal articles insurance coverage for any new valuables.

___ **Long-term care**—Do you have enough long-term care insurance coverage? This insurance keeps changing, so you need to watch it. For example, today, it's common to be insured for home health care, nursing home living, and assisted living. This was not the case several years ago, when each peril was covered by separate policies.

___ **Health and dental**—Review your health insurance and dental insurance coverage. You want to make certain your company still is financially sound. You also want to review your coverage to make sure it is adequate. Plus, you want to keep it as inexpensive as possible.

Review Your Investments

It could pay to check your investments a bit more frequently than once a year. We like to look at ours at least quarterly. On the other hand, it's not a great idea to look at them too much because that's when their ups and downs prompt you to do dumb things—like sell just because the market is down one day!

Use this checklist to review your investments:

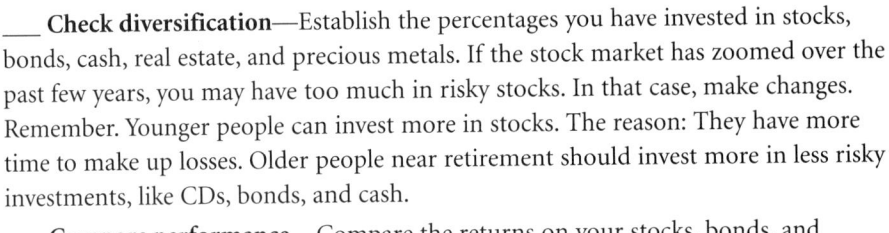

___ **Check diversification**—Establish the percentages you have invested in stocks, bonds, cash, real estate, and precious metals. If the stock market has zoomed over the past few years, you may have too much in risky stocks. In that case, make changes. Remember. Younger people can invest more in stocks. The reason: They have more time to make up losses. Older people near retirement should invest more in less risky investments, like CDs, bonds, and cash.

___ **Compare performance**—Compare the returns on your stocks, bonds, and mutual funds to similar investments and benchmarks. Own large company stocks? You might compare performance to an index like the S&P 500, which tracks the performance of 500 large companies traded on the New York Stock Exchange. Has your mutual fund, for example, seriously underperformed similar-type funds for a few years now? If so, it may be time to change.

___ **Review semi-annual and annual reports**—You might want to make changes to your mutual fund investments if the manager or managers have left a fund. You also might want to change if the management company changed, merged, or revised its strategy.

Review Your Tax Situation

Taxes can take a large chunk out of your financial life, and each year, Uncle Sam seems to tangle up our tax code more and more. Just when you think you have it nailed, something changes. Your objective is to pay as little in taxes as possible. So it's important to assess your tax situation annually—ideally before the end of the tax year so that you can make changes.

Use this checklist to assess your tax situation:

___ **Changes in the code**—Evaluate whether there have been any changes in the tax code that could affect you. For example, thinking of buying a new car? In 2006, Uncle Sam was offering a tax credit for certain hybrid vehicles—definitely an incentive. Be sure to check with your accountant.

___ **Tax breaks**—Make certain you've taken advantage of all possible retirement and savings account tax breaks. As we wrote this, there was talk in the legislature about a new tax-advantaged savings account!

___ **Income flow**—Analyze whether you're likely to have a better year income-wise this year or next year. If this is a bad year for you, it might help to accelerate any potential income into this year rather than get it next year, when you'll be in a higher tax bracket. Of course, do the opposite if you think next year will be worse income-wise.

___ **Profits and losses**—Need to sell some investments and take profits? Analyze whether you have any poor-performing investments worth selling so that you can write off losses against any gains on your income taxes.

___ **Taxable investment mix**—Determine whether you have the right mix of investments in taxable accounts versus tax-advantaged accounts. As of this writing, most advisors were recommending that, due to the relatively low 15% dividend and long-term capital gains rates on stocks, it is more advantageous for higher-tax-bracket investors to keep stocks in taxable accounts and keep bonds in tax-advantaged accounts. This could change if either the tax rules or your income tax bracket changes.

___ **Assets**—Have your assets grown substantially, or have you started a business? You might wish to evaluate whether you need to take strategies to protect your financial life from taxes and creditors. If you've started a business, for example, you might wish to have a lawyer evaluate whether a corporate structure might be advantageous.

Update Your Estate Plan

Now that your financial life is on its way to accumulating quite a bit of money, it's critical that you conduct an annual review to ensure that the people closest to you stand to benefit. Yes, once you start making lots of money, your financial life may need an estate plan. After all, you want your family or close friends to get the benefits of all your hard work when you die or if you become disabled. Again, refer to Chapter 6 for more information.

Use this list to check important aspects of your estate plan:

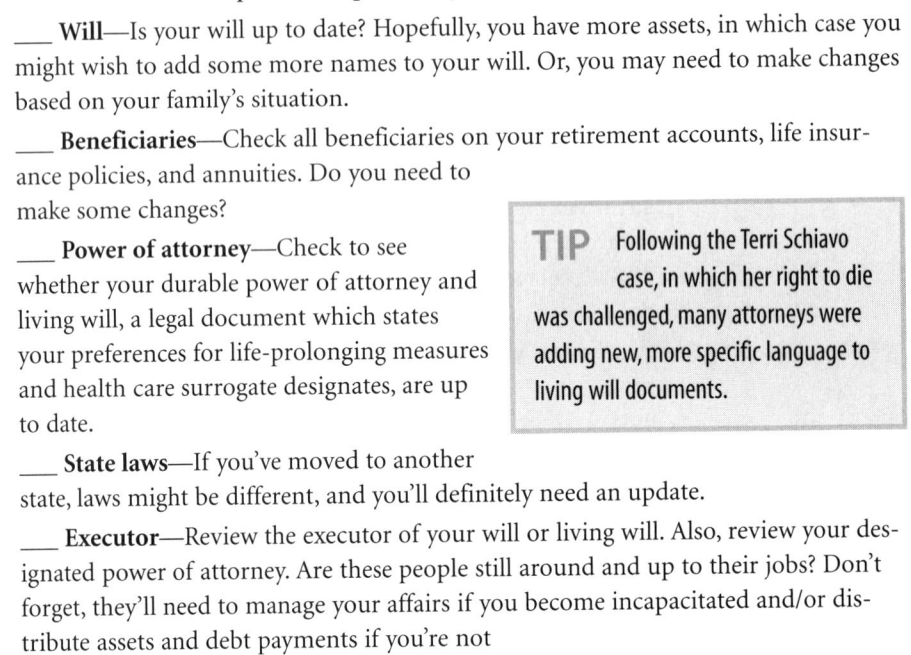

___ **Will**—Is your will up to date? Hopefully, you have more assets, in which case you might wish to add some more names to your will. Or, you may need to make changes based on your family's situation.

___ **Beneficiaries**—Check all beneficiaries on your retirement accounts, life insurance policies, and annuities. Do you need to make some changes?

___ **Power of attorney**—Check to see whether your durable power of attorney and living will, a legal document which states your preferences for life-prolonging measures and health care surrogate designates, are up to date.

> **TIP** Following the Terri Schiavo case, in which her right to die was challenged, many attorneys were adding new, more specific language to living will documents.

___ **State laws**—If you've moved to another state, laws might be different, and you'll definitely need an update.

___ **Executor**—Review the executor of your will or living will. Also, review your designated power of attorney. Are these people still around and up to their jobs? Don't forget, they'll need to manage your affairs if you become incapacitated and/or distribute assets and debt payments if you're not around.

___ **Trusts**—Evaluate with an attorney whether it pays to have a trust, which is a legal document often used to shelter assets from taxes or probate. Already have a trust? Re-examine your trust documents to see if any changes need to be made. You also may need to consult your attorney to see if estate tax rules have changed. At this writing, the estate tax was slated to be eliminated in 2010, but reinstated the following year.

> **NOTE** It could pay to consider a revocable living trust if you have at least $100,000 in assets. Reason: Due to fraud, many financial institutions today are reluctant to accept power of attorney documents. So if you were to become incapacitated, your designee still could face obstacles handling your financial affairs. Don't want a trust? At least check with all your financial institutions to see what documents they require for an appointee to handle your financial affairs. Make certain they're completed and on file.

___ **Elder care**—Do you have a plan in case you must go into a nursing home? If you don't have long-term care insurance, you might wish to visit with an elder law attorney, who can assist you with planning for Medicaid, the public assistance program that funds nursing home and health care for the poor.

This is a lot of stuff to do at once. We suggest taking a few weeks to go over all this material at least once per year.

Enjoy Your Great New Financial Life

As you might have gathered in this book, the key to having a great financial life is planning. Once you've established where you're going financially, and you're on your way, you need to give yourself some regular checkups. Your plans may need some tweaking.

> **TIP** One easy way to keep on top of your investments is to purchase some personal finance software like Microsoft Money or Quicken Premier Personal Finance software. Half the battle is entering the information. Once that's over, you just turn on your computer and click!

Savvy Spending

If you need some help, it might be a good idea to hire an experienced financial planner.

But don't lose sight of the reason you've structured a good financial life for yourself. It's to give you some enjoyment. That includes having fun right now—especially while you're still young enough to enjoy it! Plus, don't forget to take care of your spiritual self. After all, if you're too fanatical about saving money, you'll make yourself and those around you miserable. Even though you might have evolved into a great money manager, it doesn't do much good if nobody wants to associate with you!

That's why it's important to build some fun into your financial life. Our suggestion: Meet with your family members regularly. Discuss what's important for them to spend money on right now. Then, be sure that your list of financial goals includes these objectives. You all can brainstorm, perhaps together, on how you can achieve these desires at the lowest possible cost.

This exercise can improve family communication. It also can go a long way to making sure money is there—not only when you need it, but also when you don't necessarily need it. Plus, there's no better feeling in life than achieving your goals—whatever they might be. No one else is going to do it for you.

Summary

In this chapter, you learned the importance of conducting periodic examinations of your financial life. You might wish to evaluate your investments quarterly. The rest of the exercises may be conducted once a year. Examine your income and expenses to determine whether you are financially afloat. See whether there are any new ways you can cut expenses and boost income. Check to see whether your financial goals have changed. Examine your insurance, whether it is adequate, and whether your insurance company or companies still are strong. Also determine whether there are any new tax-smart moves you can make.

As you get more assets, which we hope you do, you need to consider an estate plan, so that all your hard-earned and planned-for money winds up with the right people.

Last but not least, it's important not to become too fanatical. Work into your financial goals a certain amount of money for you and your family to have fun with right now!

Once you've mastered our quick steps toward a great financial life, expect to be overcome with renewed positive energy. Spend it relaxing, socializing with family and friends, and finding meaningful, albeit lower-cost things to do. Then, sit back, and watch your great financial life get even better!

IV

Appendixes

A   References and Resources 147

B   Finding the Right Help 157

C   Mortgage Shopping Worksheet 163

References and Resources

Here's a quick reference to help you on the way to financial stability. You will find calculators to aid you with exercises outlined in the book, as well as agencies, organizations, and companies that can provide you with additional information. There also are tools and references to help you evaluate financial services. Plus, you'll find regulatory agencies to contact if you have a problem with a financial services provider or individual.

Online Calculators

- www.choosetosave.org
- www.bankrate.com
- www.myfico.com (click on Calculators at the top of the page)
- www.finance.cch.com
- http://money.cnn.com (click on Calculators at the bottom of the page)
- www.smartmoney.com/worksheets
- www.dinkytown.net

Net Worth Calculator

- www.americasaves.org (click on Savers Resources, and then Personal Wealth Estimator)

Goal Calculator

- http://alaskaadvantage.state.ak.us/calc/savings.html

College Cost Calculators

- www.collegeboard.com (click on As Parent or Student, and then click on Pay for College)
- www.finaid.com

Retirement Savings Calculators

- www.bloomberg.com (choose Calculators from the Investment Tools menu)
- www.aarp.org/money/financial_planning

Home Loan or Home Buying Calculators

- www.mtgprofessor.com (click on Calculators in the list on the left)
- www.hsh.com
- www.realtor.com (click on the Home Finance tab)
- www.mortgageunderwriters.com (click on Calculators and Tools on the left)
- www.ginniemae.gov
- http://jeacle.ie/mortgage

Disability Insurance

- www.life-line.org/disabilitycalculator

Search Engines

- www.google.com
- www.ask.com
- www.yahoo.com
- www.altavista.com
- www.lycos.com
- www.metacrawler.com
- www.msn.com
- www.dogpile.com

Low Down-Payment and Low-Cost Government Mortgage Programs

- www.hud.gov (U.S. Department of Housing and Urban Development)
- www.fha.gov
- www.homeloans.va.gov (Veterans' Affairs home loans)
- www.ncsha.org (National Council of State Housing Agencies)

Credit Card Best Deals

- www.cardweb.com
- www.bankrate.com

Money Market Mutual Fund Yields

- www.imoneynet.com

Scholarships and Loan Sources

- www.fafsa.ed.gov (federal aid application and information)
- www.ed.gov (U.S. Department of Education)
- www.learnandserve.org

- www.teri.org (TERI alternative loans)
- www.finaid.com
- www.fastweb.com
- www.srnexpress.com
- www.savingforcollege.com

529 College Savings Plans

- www.savingforcollege.com
- www.independent529plan.org, (888) 718-7878

Reverse Mortgage Information

- www.reverse.org (AARP's independent information on reverse mortgages)
- www.reversemortgage.org (website of the National Reverse Mortgage Lenders Association)

Taxes

- www.irs.gov (Internal Revenue Service)
- www.finance.cch.com (published by CCH, Inc., a tax publisher and software provider)

New and Used Car Prices

- www.kbb.com (Kelley Blue Book)
- www.edmunds.com (Edmunds)
- www.nada.com (National Automobile Dealers Association)

Consumer Reports

- www.consumerreports.org/cro/index.htm

Car Leasing

- www.bloomberg.com (click on Calculators under Investment Tools, and then click on Lease vs. Buy)

Home Buying

- www.realtor.com (property listings)
- www.zillow.com (comparative market analysis)

Attorneys

- www.martindale.com (biographical information)
- www.abanet.org (for attorneys nationally)

Elder Law

- www.naela.org (National Academy of Elder Law Attorneys)
- www.nelf.org (National Elder Law Foundation)

Consumer Law

- www.naca.net (National Association of Consumer Advocates)

Marital Law

- www.aaml.org (American Academy of Matrimonial Lawyers, (312) 263-6477)

Low-Load Life Insurance

- www.tiaa-cref.org, (877) 276-9429
- www.ameritasdirect.com (Ameritas Direct, [800] 555-4655)

COBRA Insurance Information

- www.dol.gov/dol/topic/health-plans/cobra.htm

Insurance Safety Rating Agencies

- www.moodys.com, 212-553-0300
- www.standardandpoors.com, 212-438-2400
- www.ambest.com, 908-439-2200
- www.TheStreet.com/ratings, (800) 289-9222
- www.fitchratings.com, (800) 893-4824

No-Load Mutual Fund Families

- www.mfea.com (Mutual Fund Education Alliance)
- www.vanguard.com (Vanguard Group)
- www.fidelity.com (Fidelity Investments)
- www.troweprice.com (T. Rowe Price)
- www.americancentury.com (American Century Investments)

Mutual Funds Information and Analysis

- www.morningstar.com
- http://finance.yahoo.com
- www.marketwatch.com

Purchase U.S. Treasury Securities

- www.treasurydirect.gov

Check for Complaints Against a Person or Business

- www.ripoffreport.com
- www.consumeraffairs.com

- www.complaints.com
- www.bbb.org
- www.naag.org (for a list of state attorneys general)

Credit Reports and Credit Scoring

- www.annualcreditreport.com (order a free annual credit report from each of the three major credit bureaus, [877] 322-8228)

Consumer Credit Reporting Agencies

To receive a credit report for a fee or correct an error:
- www.equifax.com (Equifax, [800] 685-1111)
- www.experian.com (Experian, [888] 397-3742)
- www.transunion.com (TransUnion, [800] 888-4213)

Largest Credit Scoring Provider

- www.myfico.com (Fair Isaac Corporation, [800] 319-4433)

Help with Debt

- www.debtorsanonymous.org (Debtors Anonymous)
- www.nfcc.org (National Foundation for Credit Counseling, [800] 388-2227)
- www.aiccca.org (Association of Independent Consumer Credit Counseling Agencies, [800] 450-1794)

Bankruptcy Information

- www.usdoj.gov/ust (U.S. Department of Justice Trustee Program)

Fraud

- www.naag.org (National Association of Attorneys General)

Insurance Information

- www.iii.org (Insurance Information Institute)

Social Security Administration

- www.ssa.gov

Unclaimed Property

- www.missingmoney.com (website set up by the National Association of Unclaimed Property Administrators)

Consumer Expenditures

- www.epi.org (Economic Policy Institute)

Economic Statistics and Salary Data

- www.bls.gov (Bureau of Labor Statistics)

Financial Regulators

- www.sec.gov (Securities and Exchange Commission, 202-551-6551)
- www.naic.org (National Association of Insurance Commissioners, 816-842-3600)
- www.nasaa.org (North American Securities Administrators Association, 202-737-0900)
- www.nasd.com (National Association of Securities Dealers, 202-728-8000)
- www.csbs.org (Conference of State Bank Supervisors, 202-296-2840)

APPENDIX A   References and Resources

- www.federalreserve.gov, 202-452-3693
- www.fdic.gov, (877) 275-3342
- www.ftc.gov/ftc/consumer.htm (Federal Trade Commission, [877] 382-4357)
- www.ncua.gov (National Credit Union Administration, 703-518-6330)
- www.occ.treas.gov (Office of the Comptroller of the Currency, [800] 613-6743)
- www.ots.treas.gov (Office of Thrift Supervision, [800] 842-6929)

B

Finding the Right Help

If you still feel uncomfortable managing your money, an experienced financial advisor or debt counselor may help. Unfortunately, not all have your interests at heart. Anytime you seek help, you always need to do two things:

- Make certain the person you consider is legitimate. Check out proper licenses and designations. There are too many stories of con artists who say they're financial professionals and walk off with people's money! Also, search for complaints against the person. We gave you some places to go to check people out in Appendix A, "References and Resources."
- Determine how you will be charged, and exactly what the professional you're considering will do for the money.

In this appendix, we give you some other points to consider.

Getting Good Investment Help

When it comes to picking a financial advisor, how you pay is a controversial issue. An advisor may be paid in one of three ways:

- Strictly by you—through either a flat fee or an annual fee based on the amount of your assets he or she has under management
- By straight commission
- A combination of these methods

So, where do you start?

Narrow your quest for a financial advisor by checking out a couple of websites:

- **www.napfa.org**—This is the website of the National Association of Personal Financial Advisors (NAPFA). Members of that organization are required to be paid a fee only by their clients.
- **www.fpanet.org**—This is the website for the Financial Planning Association.

As we indicated in Appendix A, you can check the background of a financial advisor at www.sec.gov, www.nasaa.org, www.nasd.com, and www.cfpboard.org.

TIP Also use Internet search engines, which we listed in Appendix A, to locate other possible financial advisors in your area. Often, biographical information is listed on advisor websites.

Following are issues to consider in evaluating a candidate:

- How much will he or she charge and how? Who pays him or her?
- What will he or she do for the money?
- Will the advisor provide you with a financial plan?
- How frequently will he or she review your situation to consider adjustments to your investments?
- What steps will the advisor take to minimize your taxes?
- How long has the advisor been in business?
- What type of business is the advisor in? Does the advisor deal with clients whose net worth is similar to yours?

- What letter designations does the advisor have and do they jive with your needs? As we also mentioned in Chapter 6, "Protecting the Downside: Insurance and Other Safeguards," CLU and ChFC, for example, indicate heavy training in insurance and financial planning; PFS may indicate the advisor's primary profession is accounting; and CFP indicates the advisor met requirements set by the CFP Board for overall financial planning. You want to examine all candidates' educational backgrounds.
- What other credentials does the advisor have? Some might also be attorneys or accountants.

Interview some of the advisor's past and existing clients to find the financial professional's strengths and weaknesses.

Can't afford to hire a financial advisor? Check out these options:

- **www.consultaplanner.org**—This website is sponsored by six of the nation's leading financial planning groups who have teamed up with a host of charities. It offers free financial guidance to those who can't afford a financial advisor.
- **www.fpaprobono.org**—Through the Financial Planning Association, you can find advisors volunteering their time.
- **www.myfinancialadvice.com**—This Denver-based company connects consumers with financial advisors nationwide. Have a specific question? You can arrange a phone call or email to receive the advisor's proposal and cost of the telephone call.
- **www.garrettplanningnetwork.com**—This network charges hourly fees.

Getting Credit Counseling

Need a credit counseling agency? Get referrals from area universities, banks, military bases, credit unions, or housing authorities.

The National Consumer Law Center, Boston, has warned that because funding has been cut for nonprofit credit counseling services, some agencies, though nonprofit, behave too much like for-profit agencies.

CAUTION While credit counseling advice used to come cheap, more are charging higher fees. Also, there historically have been problems with consumers being defrauded by agencies.

The Federal Trade Commission (FTC) suggests that before you sign onto any debt management program, be sure to get the terms, including fees, in writing. Avoid agencies whose counselors are paid solely on commission. Ask these questions of any credit counseling agency:

- What services do you offer?
- Will you help me develop a plan for avoiding problems in the future?
- What are your fees?
- What if I can't afford to pay your fees?
- Are you licensed to offer services in my state?
- What are the qualifications of your counselors? Are they accredited or certified by an outside organization? What training do they receive?
- What do you to do keep information about me (including my address, phone number, and financial information) confidential and secure?
- How are your employees paid? Are they paid more if I sign up for certain services, if I pay a fee, or make a contribution to your organization?
- Suppose I want only the credit counseling services and budget analysis that are required before I can file for bankruptcy relief. How much will these services cost? What services will your company provide? How will I know that I have the correct certificate I need to file for bankruptcy? Does the certificate cost extra? If so, how much?

As we told you in Chapter 3, "Zeroing In on Your Debt," major national credit counseling networks include The National Foundation for Credit Counseling and The Association of Independent Consumer Credit Counseling Agencies. You can find their contact information in Appendix A.

To check whether a credit counseling agency you're considering is government approved for bankruptcy, visit www.usdoj.gov/ust.

> **CAUTION** Beware if you may need to file bankruptcy. You're required to see a government-approved credit counselor within six months before you file. This requirement temporarily has been waived for victims of Hurricanes Katrina and Rita.

If you do sign up for a debt management plan—in which the credit counseling agency gets approval to make payments to your creditors—confirm with your creditors that payments are being made. The FTC advises that you

- Make regular, timely payments.
- Always read your monthly statements promptly to make sure your creditors are getting paid according to your plan.
- Contact the organization responsible for your plan if you can't make a scheduled payment.

If your credit counseling agency goes out of business, the FTC says to

- Contact your bank to stop payment if you're making your payments through automatic withdrawal.
- Start paying bills directly to your creditors.
- Notify your creditors that the organization handling your program is going out of business.
- Consider working out a payment plan with creditors yourself. Ask if they will cut your interest rate without a debt management program.
- Order a copy of your credit report at www.annualcreditreport.com. Check for late payments or missed debt management plan payments that might have resulted from the company going out of business. If you see any "late" notations, call your creditor immediately, explain the circumstances, and ask that it be removed. However, the creditor has no obligation to remove it.

For more information on your credit rights, visit www.ftc.gov.

Mortgage Shopping Worksheet

	Lender 1		Lender 2	
	Mortgage 1	Mortgage 2	Mortgage 1	Mortgage 2
Name of Lender				
Name of Contact				
Date of Contact				
Mortgage Amount				

Basic Information on the Loans

Type of mortgage: fixed rate, adjustable rate, conventional, FHA, other? If adjustable, see below.				
Minimum down payment required				
Loan term (length of loan)				
Contract interest rate				
Annual percentage rate (APR)				
Points (may be called loan discount points)				
Monthly private mortgage insurance (PMI) premiums				
How long must you keep PMI?				
Estimated monthly escrow for taxes and hazard insurance				
Estimated monthly payment (principal, interest, taxes, insurance, PMI)				

Fees (different institutions may have different names for some fees and may charge different fees; we have listed some typical fees you may see on loan documents)

Application fee or loan-processing fee				
Origination fee or underwriting fee				
Lender fee or funding fee				
Appraisal fee				

APPENDIX C Mortgage Shopping Worksheet

	Lender 1		Lender 2	
	Mortgage 1	Mortgage 2	Mortgage 1	Mortgage 2
Application fee or loan-processing fee				
Attorney fees				
Document preparation and recording fees				
Broker fees (may be quoted as points, origination fees, or interest rate add-on)				
Credit report fee				
Other fees				

Other Costs at Closing/Settlement

	Lender 1		Lender 2	
	Mortgage 1	Mortgage 2	Mortgage 1	Mortgage 2
Title search/title insurance				
For lender				
For you				
Estimated prepaid amounts for interest, taxes, hazard insurance, payments to escrow				
State and local taxes, stamp taxes, transfer taxes				
Flood determination				
Prepaid PMI				
Surveys and home inspections				
Total Fees and Other Closing/Settlement Cost Estimates				

Other Questions and Considerations About the Loan

Are any of the fees or costs waivable?

	Lender 1		Lender 2	
	Mortgage 1	Mortgage 2	Mortgage 1	Mortgage 2
Prepayment Penalties				
Is there a prepayment penalty?				
If so, how much is it?				
How long does the penalty period last (for example, 3 years, 5 years)?				
Are extra principal payments allowed?				
Lock-ins				
Is the lock-in agreement in writing?				
Is there a fee to lock in?				
When does the lock-in occur—at application, approval, or another time?				
How long will the lock-in last?				
If the rate drops before closing, can you lock in at a lower rate?				
If the Loan Is an Adjustable-Rate Mortgage				
What is the initial rate?				
What is the maximum the rate could be next year?				
What are the rate and payment caps each year and over the life of the loan?				
What is the frequency of rate change and of any changes to the monthly payment?				
What is the index that the lender will use?				
What margin will the lender add to the index?				

APPENDIX C Mortgage Shopping Worksheet

	Lender 1		Lender 2	
	Mortgage 1	Mortgage 2	Mortgage 1	Mortgage 2
Credit Life Insurance				
Does the monthly amount quoted to you include a charge for credit life insurance?				
If so, does the lender require credit life insurance as a condition of the loan?				
How much does the credit life insurance cost?				
How much lower would your monthly payment be without the credit life insurance?				
If the lender does not require credit life insurance, and you still want to buy it, what rates can you get from other insurance providers?				

Sources:
Department of Housing and Urban Development
Department of Justice
Department of the Treasury
Federal Deposit Insurance Corporation
Federal Housing Finance Board
Federal Reserve Board
Federal Trade Commission
National Credit Union Administration
Office of Federal Housing Enterprise Oversight
Office of the Comptroller of the Currency
Office of Thrift Supervision

Index

NUMBERS

15-year fixed rate mortgages, 129
40-50 year mortgages, 129
401(k)s, 98-100
529 plans, 111-113

A

actively managed mutual funds, 72-73
adjustable-rate mortgages, 128
amortization (mortgages), 127
annuities
    IRAs versus, 103
    no-load, 102
    retirement, 101
        deferred fixed, 102
        deferred variable, 102
        immediate, 102-103
appraisal fees (mortgages), 127
assets
    determining, 9
    subtracting
        debts from (determining net worth), 11
        liabilities from (determining net worth), 11
attorneys
    consumer law, 151
    elder law, 151
    marital law, 151
    power of,
        estate plans, 142
        wills, 90
    web resources, 151

automobiles
    insurance, 88-90
    leases, 125, 151
    loans, 125-126
        strategies for, 132-133
        web resources, 150

B

babies, financial planning, 30-31
balanced funds, 70
balloon mortgages, 129
bankruptcy
    declaring, 38-39
    web resources, 153
banks
    deposits, low-risk investments, 62-63
    out-of-town banking, 63
beneficiaries (estate plans), 142
benefits, tracking, 21
big purchases, planning, 28-30
biweekly mortgages (debt elimination), 135
bonds
    college investments, 116
    corporate, 66
    investments, 53
    laddering, 66
    low-risk investments, 65-67
    municipal, 66
    savings, 64
    treasury, 64
bottom line, determining, 8
    assets
        determining, 9
        subtracting debts from, 11
        subtracting liabilities from, 11

debts
  listing, 10-11
  subtracting from assets, 11
liabilities
  listing, 10-11
  subtracting from assets, 11
  net worth calculator websites, 9
budget calculator websites, 17
Bureau of Labor Statistics website, salary information, 20
business complaint websites, 152

C

calculators (online), 147
  college cost, 148
  disability insurance, 148
  goal, 148
  home loans, 148
  net worth, 148
  retirement savings, 148
capitalization (stocks), 67
cars
  insurance, 88-90
  leases, 125, 151
  loans, 125-126
    strategies for, 132-133
    web resources, 150
cash
  investments, 52
  quick cash, freeing up
    controlling debt, 17
    increasing income, 20-21
    trimming expenses, 17-19
CCH Financial Planning Toolkit, personal finance calculators, 12
CDs
  laddering, 63
  low-risk investments, 62-63
  out-of-town banks, buying from, 63
CFP (Certified Financial Planners), 86
children, financial planning
  babies, 30-31
  education, 32
closing costs (mortgages), 126
CLU (Chartered Life Underwriters), 86

CNNMoney.com website
  net worth calculators, 9
  personal finance calculators, 12
COBRA (Consolidated Omnibus Budget Reconciliation Act), 82, 152
collateralized bank loans, 131
collections (debt), protection from, 34
college
  alternative strategies to paying for, 118
  cost calculators, 148
  costs, determining, 110
  financial aid, 21, 116-117
  investment options
    529 plans, 111-113
    Coverdell ESAs, 113
    IRAs, 114
    rules for, 116
    savings bonds, 114
    Uniform Gifts to Minors Act, 113
    Uniform Transfers to Minors Act, 113
  loans, 118
  planning for, 32
  saving for, 111-113, 150
  scholarships, 116-117, 149-150
  tax breaks
    Hope Scholarship credits, 115
    Lifetime Learning credits, 115
    student loan tax deductions, 115
commissions (mutual funds), 71
community service, paying for college, 118
company pension loans, 132
consolidating debt, 37-38
Consumer Federation of America life insurance evaluation website, 86
consumer law, web resources, 151
consumer reports website, 150
corporate bonds, 66
cost calculator websites, setting financial goals, 25-26
counseling (credit), 159-161
Coverdell ESA (Educational Savings Accounts), 113
credit, paying for college, 118

credit cards
  benefits of, 122
  credit records, establishing/rebuilding, 124
  debt
    consolidating, 37
    self-control, 35
  terms of agreement, 123-124
  web resources, 149
credit counseling, 36, 159-161
credit lines, home equity, 131
credit reports
  correcting, 44-45
  viewing, 42-43
  web resources, 153
  websites, 43
credit score
  bad scores, 45-46
  determining, 39-42
  improving, 42-43, 46
  web resources, 153
  websites, 41

D

debt
  bankruptcy, declaring, 38-39
  collectors, protection from, 34
  consolidating, 37-38
  controlling, 17
  credit reports
    correcting, 44-45
    viewing, 42-43
  credit score
    bad scores, 45-46
    determining, 39-42
    improving, 42-43, 46
  determining reasons for, 34
  eliminating
    biweekly mortgages, 135
    credit counseling, 36, 159-161
    prepaying mortgages, 134
    refinancing homes, 133
    self-control, 35
    web resources, 153, 160-161
  listing (determining net worth), 10-11
  subtracting from assets (determining net worth), 11

Debt Collection Practices Act, 34
deferred fixed annuities, 102
deferred variable annuities, 102
deposits (bank), low-risk investments, 62-63
designation of health care surrogate documents (wills), 90
disability benefits, tracking, 21
disability insurance, 82-83, 148
dollar cost averaging (mutual funds), 73
downside preparedness checklist, 24
durable power of attorney (wills), 90

E

Economic Policy Institute website, 17, 154
education
    alternative strategies to paying for, 118
    costs, determining, 110, 148
    financial aid, 116-117
    investment options
        529 plans, 111-113
        Coverdell ESAs, 113
        IRAs, 114
        rules for, 116
        savings bonds, 114
        Uniform Gifts to Minors Act, 113
    loans, 118
    planning for, 32
    saving for, 111, 150
    scholarships, 116-117, 149-150
    tax breaks
        Hope Scholarship credits, 115
        Lifetime Learning credits, 115
        student loan tax deductions, 115
elder care (estate plans), 142
elder law, web resources, 151
equity loans, 131
    college, paying for, 118
    houses, 38
ESA (Educational Savings Accounts), 113
estate plans, updating, 142
EXCEL loans (college), 118
exchange-traded funds, investing in, 59-60
executors (estate plans), 142
expense ratios (mutual funds), 71
expenses
    monthly expenses, calculating, 13-14
    trimming, 17-19

F

family budget calculator websites, 17
FICO (Fair Isaac Corp.) scores. *See* credit score
financial aid (college), 21, 116-117
financial goals
    big purchases, planning, 28-30
    children, planning for
        babies, 30-31
        education, 32
    cost calculator websites, 25-26, 148
    houses, planning for, 28-30
    listing, 25
    long term
        higher-risk investments, 67
        retirement, planning for, 32
        savings plans, developing, 26-27
        setting, 15-16
    short-term goals, low-risk investments, 62-67
financial regulators, web resources, 154
fraud, web resources, 154
funds
    money, college investments, 116
    mutual
        actively managed funds, 72-73
        balanced funds, 70
        commissions, 71
        dollar cost averaging, 73
        expense ratios, 71
        increasing performance, 70-74
        index funds, 72
        life-cycle funds, 69-70
        loads, 71
        Morningstar, Inc., 69
        no-load funds, 71
        retirement, 105
        risk analysis, 68-69
        target funds, 69-70
        web resources, 71, 149, 152

G

goals (financial)
    big purchases, planning, 28-30
    children, planning for
        babies, 30-31
        education, 32
    cost calculator websites, 25-26, 148
    houses, planning for, 28-30
    listing, 25
    long-term
        higher-risk investments, 67
        retirement, planning for, 32
        savings plans, developing, 26-27
        setting, 15-16
    short-term, low-risk investments, 62-67
growth stocks, 67

H

health care power of attorney (wills), 90
health insurance, 79
    COBRA, 82
    group rates, 82
    Health Savings Accounts, 81
    high deductibles, 81
    HMO policies, 80
    indemnity policies, 80
    major medical coverage policies, 80
    PPO policies, 80
    purchasing, 81
Health Savings Accounts, 81
help, investments, 158-159
higher education
    alternative strategies to paying for, 118
    costs, determining, 110, 148
    financial aid, 116-117

higher education

investment options
    529 plans, 111-113
    Coverdell ESAs, 113
    IRAs, 114
    rules for, 116
    savings bonds, 114
    Uniform Gifts to Minors Act, 113
loans, 118
planning for, 32
saving for, 111, 150
scholarships, 116-117, 149-150
tax breaks
    Hope Scholarship credits, 115
    Lifetime Learning credits, 115
    student loan tax deductions, 115
higher-paying jobs, finding, 20
higher-risk investments, stocks, 67
HMO (health maintenance organization) policies (health insurance), 80
home equity credit lines, 131
home loans
calculators, 148
equity loans, 38, 131, 181
homeowner's insurance, 89-90
Hope Scholarship credits, 115
houses
buying
    purchase calculator websites, 30
    purchase plans, 28-30
    web resources, 151
equity credit lines, 131
insurance, 89-90
loans
    calculators, 148
    equity loans, 38, 131, 181
    strategies for, 132-133
mortgages
    debt elimination, 134-135
    reverse mortgages, 106
Real Estate Settlement Procedures Act, 41
refinancing, debt elimination, 133
web resources, 151
hybrid mortgages, 128

I

immediate annuities, 102-103
income
evaluation checklist, 138-139
increasing
    financial services, 21
    finding higher-paying jobs, 20
    finding Social Security/disability benefits, 21
    finding tax breaks, 21
    unclaimed assets, 21
monthly income, calculating, 12-15
taxes, IRA deductions, 98
income stocks, 67
indemnity policies (health insurance), 80
independent 529 plans, 112
index mutual funds, 72
insurance
disability, 82-83, 148
downside preparedness checklist, 24
evaluation checklist, 139-140
health, 79
    COBRA, 82, 152
    cost-cutting strategies, 81
    group rates, 82
    Health Savings Accounts, 81
    high deductibles, 81
    HMO policies, 80
    indemnity policies, 80
    major medical coverage policies, 80
    PPO policies, 80
    rules for purchasing, 81
leases, 126
life
    CFPs, 86
    CLUs, 86
    evaluation websites, 86
    loans against, 132
    low-load companies, 86
    PFSs, 86
    riders, 85
    term insurance policies, 84

universal life insurance policies, 85
variable life insurance policies, 85
web resources, 151
whole life insurance policies, 84
long-term care, 87-88
National Association of Insurance Commissioners website, 79
needs, determining, 24
property
    automobile, 88
    homeowner's, 89
    renter's, 89
    umbrella liability coverage, 90
purchasing
    finding financially secure companies, 78-79
    ratings company websites, 78
    rules for, 77
safety rating agency websites, 152
title insurance fees (mortgages), 127
web resources, 154
interest rate caps (adjustable-rate mortgages), 128
investments
basic rules, 54-55
bonds, 53
cash, 52
college, 111
    529 plans, 111-113
    Coverdell ESAs, 113
    IRAs, 114
    rules for, 116
    savings bonds, 114
    Uniform Gifts to Minors Act, 113
    Uniform Transfers to Minors Act, 113
exchange-traded funds, 59-60
help, 158-159
higher-risk, stocks, 67
investors, determining type of, 56-58

low-risk
   bank deposits, 62-63
   bonds, 65-67
   CDs, 62-63
   treasury securities, 64-65
mutual funds, 59-60
   actively managed funds, 72-73
   balanced funds, 70
   commissions, 71
   dollar cost averaging, 73
   expense ratios, 71
   increasing performance, 70-74
   index funds, 72
   life-cycle funds, 69-70
   loads, 71
   Morningstar, Inc., 69
   no-load funds, 71
   risk analysis, 68-69
   target funds, 69-70
   web resources, 71
rebalancing, 73-74
retirement, receiving payments during, 105
review checklist, 140
safety, 55
selecting, 58
stocks, 54
taxes, 74-75

IRAs (individual retirement accounts), 97-99
   annuities versus, 103
   college investments, 114
   income tax deductions, 98
   Roth IRAs, 100-101
   withdrawal penalties, 100

IRS (Internal Revenue Service)
   tax breaks, finding, 21
   withholdings calculator website, 21

J - K - L

jobs (higher-paying), finding, 20

laddering
   bonds, 66
   CDs, 63

large-cap stocks, 67
leases
   automobiles, 125, 151
   insurance, 126
lender recasts (mortgages), 128
liabilities (determining net worth)
   listing, 10-11
   subtracting from assets, 11
life insurance
   CFPs, 86
   CLUs, 86
   evaluation websites, 86
   loans against, 132
   low-load companies, 86
   PFSs, 86
   riders, 85
   term insurance policies, 84
   universal life insurance policies, 85
   variable life insurance policies, 85
   web resources, 151
   whole life insurance policies, 84
life-cycle funds, 69-70
Lifetime Learning credits, 115
living wills, 90
loads (mutual funds), 71
loans
   automobiles, 125-126
      strategies, 132-133
      web resources, 150
   collateralized bank, 131
   college, 115, 118
   credit cards
      benefits of, 122
      establishing/rebuilding credit record, 124
      terms of agreement, 123-124
      web resources, 149
   houses
      equity, 38, 118, 131
      loan calculators, 148
      strategies for, 132-133
   life insurance policies, 132
   margin, 132
   mortgages
      15-year fixed rate, 129
      40-50 year, 129
      adjustable rate, 128

      appraisal fees, 127
      balloon, 129
      closing costs, 126
      debt elimination, 134-135
      hybrid, 128
      lender recasts, 128
      negative amortization, 127
      option, 129
      points, 126
      shopping worksheet, 164-167
      special programs, 130
      strategies for evaluating, 129-130
      title insurance fees, 127
      web resources, 149-150
   payday, 133
   pensions, 132
   rules for obtaining, 121
   tax refund anticipation loans, 133
long-term care insurance, 87-88
long-term financial goals, higher-risk investments, 67
low-risk investments
   bank deposits, 62-63
   bonds, 65-67
   CDs, 62-63
   treasury securities, 64-65

M

major medical coverage policies (health insurance), 80
margin loans, 132
marital law, web resources, 151
mid-cap stocks, 67
missingmoney.com website, 21
money, changing attitudes on, 15
money funds, college investments, 116
monthly expenses, calculating, 13-14
monthly income, calculating, 12-15
Morningstar, Inc., mutual funds, 69
mortgages
   15-year fixed rate, 129
   40-50 year, 129
   adjustable-rate, 128
   appraisal fees, 127

How can we make this index more useful? Email us at indexes@quepublishing.com

mortgages

  balloon, 129
  biweekly, debt elimination, 135
  calculators, 148
  closing costs, 126
  evaluating, strategies for, 129-130
  hybrid, 128
  lender recasts, 128
  negative amortization, 127
  option, 129
  points, 126
  prepaying, debt elimination, 134
  reverse, 106
  shopping worksheet, 164-167
  special programs, 130
  title insurance fees, 127
  web resources, 149-150
municipal bonds, 66
mutual funds
  actively managed funds, 72-73
  balanced funds, 70
  commissions, 71
  dollar cost averaging, 73
  expense ratios, 71
  index funds, 72
  investing in, 59-60
  life-cycle funds, 69-70
  loads, 71
  Morningstar, Inc., 69
  no-load funds, 71
  performance, increasing, 70-74
  retirement, 105
  risk analysis, 68-69
  target funds, 69-70
  web resources, 71, 149, 152

N

National Association of Insurance Commissioners website, 78
negative amortization (mortgages), 127
net worth calculators, 148
net worth, determining, 8
  assets
    determining, 9
    subtracting debts from, 11
    subtracting liabilities from, 11
  calculators, 9, 148

  debts
    listing, 10-11
    subtracting from assets, 11
  liabilities
    listing, 10-11
    subtracting from assets, 11
no-load annuities, 102
no-load mutual funds, 71
notes (treasury), terms of, 64

O - P

online calculators, 147
  college cost, 148
  disability insurance, 148
  goal, 148
  home loans, 148
  net worth, 148
  retirement savings, 148
option mortgages, 129
out-of-town banking, 63

payday loans, 133
pension loans, 132
personal finance calculator websites, 12
PFS (Personal Financial Specialists), 86
PLUS loans (college), 118
points (mortgages), 126
power of attorney
  estate plans, 142
  wills, 90
PPO (preferred provider organization) policies (health insurance), 80
prepaid tuition plans (529 plans), 112
prepaying mortgages (debt elimination), 134
property insurance
  automobile, 88
  homeowner's, 89
  renter's, 89
  umbrella liability coverage, 90

Q - R

quick cash, freeing up
  controlling debt, 17
  increasing income
    financial aid, 21
    finding higher-paying jobs, 20
    finding Social Security/disability benefits, 21
    finding tax breaks, 21
    unclaimed assets, 21
  trimming expenses, 17-19

rate adjustments (adjustable-rate mortgages), 128
rate floors (adjustable-rate mortgages), 128
Real Estate Settlement Procedures Act, 41
rebalancing investments, 73-74
rebuilding credit records, 124
refinancing homes (debt elimination), 133
refund anticipation loans (taxes), 133
renter's insurance, 89
retirement
  401(k)s, 98-100
  annual income from retirement assets table, 104
  annuities, 101
    deferred fixed, 102
    deferred variable, 102
    immediate, 102-103
    IRAs versus, 103
    no-load, 102
  cost management strategies, 106
  expenses during retirement table, 104
  expenses, determining, 104
  income, determining, 96-97, 104
  investments, withdrawing from, 105
  IRAs, 97-99
    annuities versus, 103
    income tax deductions, 98
    Roth IRAs, 100-101
    withdrawal penalties, 100

monthly investment table, 97
mutual funds, 105
planning for, 32
reverse mortgages, 106
savings calculators, 148
SEPs, 97, 101
SIMPLE plans, 101
stock dividends, 105
transferring plans, 101
reverse mortgages, 106
riders (life insurance), 85
ROTC (Reserve Officers' Training Corps), paying for college, 118
Roth IRAs (individual retirement arrangements), 100-101

S

salaries
informational websites, 20
statistics web resources, 154
salary reduction plans. *See* **401(k)s**
savings bonds
college investments, 114
minimums of, 64
terms of, 64
savings plans, developing, 26-27
scholarships, 116-117, 149-150
search engines, 149
securities (treasury)
low-risk investments, 64-65
taxes, 65
TIPS, 64
web resources, 152
SEPs (simplified employee pensions), 97, 101
short-term financial goals, low-risk investments
bank deposits, 62-63
bonds, 65-67
treasury securities, 64-65
signature loans (college), 118
SIMPLE plans (Savings Incentive Match Plan for Employees), 101
small businesses, retirement plans, 101

small-cap stocks, 67
SmartMoney.com website, net worth calculators, 9
Social Security, 82-83
benefits, tracking, 21
Uniform Gifts to Minors Act, 113
Uniform Transfers to Minors Act, 113
web resources, 154
spending
cutting, 18-19
evaluation checklist, 138-139
SSI (Supplemental Security Income), 82-83
Stafford loans, 118
stocks
capitalization, 67
college investments, 116
growth, 67
higher-risk investments, 67
income, 67
investments, 54
retirement, 105
value, 67
student loans, interest tax deductions, 115

T

target funds, 69-70
taxes
annuities, 101
deferred fixed, 102
deferred variable, 102
immediate, 102
breaks, finding, 21
college, breaks for
Hope Scholarship credits, 115
Lifetime Learning credits, 115
student loan tax deductions, 115
income, IRA deductions, 98
investments, 74-75
refund anticipation loans, 133
review checklist, 141
treasury securities, 65
Uniform Gifts to Minors Act, 113

Uniform Transfers to Minors Act, 113
web resources, 150
withholdings calculator website, 21
TERI alternative loans (college), 118
term insurance policies (life insurance), 84
terms of agreement (credit cards), 123-124
TIPS (Treasury Inflation-Protected Securities), 64
title insurance fees (mortgages), 127
treasury securities
low-risk investments, 64-65
taxes, 65
TIPS, 64
web resources, 152
trusts, estate plans, 142

U - V

umbrella liability coverage (property insurance), 90
unclaimed assets websites, 21
unclaimed property, web resources, 154
Uniform Gifts to Minors Act, 113
Uniform Transfers to Minors Act, 113
universal life insurance policies, 85
updating estate plans, 142
upfront points (mortgages), 126
U.S. savings bonds, 64
U.S. treasury securities
low-risk investments, 64-65
taxes, 65
TIPS, 64
web resources, 152

value stocks, 67
variable life insurance policies (life insurance), 85
veterans benefits, tracking, 21

How can we make this index more useful? Email us at indexes@quepublishing.com

W - X - Y - Z

web resources
    attorneys, 151
    automobiles
        leases, 151
        loans, 150
    bankruptcy, 153
    business complaints, 152
    college
        savings plans, 150
        scholarships, 149
    consumer law, 151
    consumer reports website, 150
    credit counseling, 160-161
    credit reports, 153
    credit scores, 153
    debt, eliminating, 153
    elder law, 151
    financial regulators, 154
    fraud, 154
    houses, 151
    insurance, 154
        COBRA, 152
        life, 151
        safety rating agencies, 152
    investments, help, 158-159
    loans
        credit cards, 149
        marital law, 151
        mortgages, 149-150
        mutual funds, 149, 152
    online calculators, 147
        college cost, 148
        disability insurance, 148
        goal, 148
        home loans, 148
        net worth, 148
        retirement savings, 148
    salary statistics, 154
    search engines, 149
    securities, 152
    social security, 154
    taxes, 150
    unclaimed property, 154

websites
    benefits, tracking, 21
    cost calculators, setting financial goals, 25-26
    credit reports, 43
    credit scores, obtaining, 41
    debt collection, protection from, 34
    family budget calculators, 17
    financial aid, 21
    housing purchase calculators, 30
    net worth calculators, 9
    personal finance calculators, 12
    salary information, 20
    unclaimed assets, 21
    withholdings calculator (taxes), 21

whole life insurance policies, 84
wills, 142
    designation of health care surrogate documents, 90
    durable power of attorney, 90
    living, 90